TRANSFORMING SCRIPTURES

TRANSFORMING SCRIPTURE

KATHERINE CLAY BASSARD

transforming scriptures

AFRICAN AMERICAN WOMEN

WRITERS AND THE BIBLE

The University of Georgia Press   Athens and London

Paperback edition published in 2011 by
The University of Georgia Press
Athens, Georgia 30602
www.ugapress.org
© 2010 by Katherine Clay Bassard
All rights reserved
Designed by Mindy Basinger Hill
Set in 10/13 Minion Pro
Printed digitally in the United States of
America

The Library of Congress has cataloged the
hardcover edition of this book as follows:
Bassard, Katherine Clay, 1959–
Transforming scriptures : African American
women writers and the Bible / Katherine Clay
Bassard.
viii, 166 p. ; 24 cm.
Includes bibliographical references
(p. [143]–152) and indexes.
ISBN-13: 978-0-8203-3090-7 (hardcover)
ISBN-10: 0-8203-3090-6 (hardcover)
1. Bible—In literature. 2. American literature—
African American authors—History and
criticism. 3. American literature—Women
authors—History and criticism. 4. African
American women—Religion. 5. African
American women in literature. I. Title.
PS153.N5B34 2010
810.9'3822082—dc22   2009032883

Paperback ISBN-13: 978-0-8203-3880-4
          ISBN-10: 0-8203-3880-X

British Library Cataloging-in-Publication
Data available

Portions of chapter 2 previously appeared as
"Private Interpretations: The Defense of Slavery, Nineteenth-Century Hermeneutics, and the Poetry of Frances E. W. Harper" in *There Before Us: Religion, Literature, and Culture from Emerson to Wendell Berry*, ed. Roger Lundin, 110–40 (Grand Rapids, Mich.: Wm. B. Eerdmans Publishing Co., 2007). © 2007 Wm. B. Eerdmans Publishing Company, Grand Rapids, Mich. Reprinted by permission of the publisher. All rights reserved.

An earlier version of chapter 5 appeared as "'Beyond Mortal Vision': Harriet E. Wilson's *Our Nig* and the American Racial Dream-Text" in *Female Subjects in Black and White: Race, Psychoanalysis, Feminism*, ed. Elizabeth Abel, Barbara Christian, and Helene Moglen, 187–200 (Berkeley: University of California Press, 1997). Reprinted by permission of the publisher.

contents

vii   Acknowledgments

1   **INTRODUCTION.** The Bible and African American Women Writers: A Literary Witness

6   **PART ONE. TROUBLING HERMENEUTICS**

9   **CHAPTER ONE.** Talking Mules and Troubled Hermeneutics: Black Women's Biblical Self-Disclosures

25   **CHAPTER TWO.** Private Interpretations: The Bible Defense of Slavery and Nineteenth-Century Racial Hermeneutics

48   **PART TWO. TRANSFORMING SCRIPTURES**

51   **CHAPTER THREE.** Sampling the Scriptures: Maria W. Stewart and the Genre of Prayer

67   **CHAPTER FOUR.** Hannah's Craft: Biblical Passing in *The Bondwoman's Narrative*

79   **CHAPTER FIVE.** "Beyond Mortal Vision": Identification and Miscegenation in the Joseph Cycle and Harriet E. Wilson's *Our Nig*

93   **CHAPTER SIX.** And the Greatest of These: *Eros, Philos,* and *Agape* in Two Contemporary Black Women's Novels

107   Appendix

133   Notes

143   Bibliography

153   Index of Scriptural References

159   General Index

acknowledgments

※ Verbum Domini
   Deo gratias!

As with any project that one has worked on for the better part of a decade, I owe thanks to numerous people scattered abroad in many locations. Funding by a Pew Evangelical Scholars grant (1999–2000), a Ford Foundation Post-Doctoral Fellowship (1998–99), and residencies at the Graduate Theological Union in Berkeley, California (1998–99), and the Virginia Center for the Humanities in Charlottesville, Virginia (Fall 2005), were essential in providing the time and space to work. Thanks are also owed to Virginia Commonwealth University for a Career Development Enhancement Grant (Spring and Summer 2008) and course relief to finish the manuscript.

Alaina Hohnarth, my research assistant, was invaluable throughout the final year of manuscript preparation and research. Undergraduate and graduate students in various classes—"The Bible as Literature" and "Bible and Literary Theory" at UC Berkeley, "Bible and African American Literature" at VCU, and a summer graduate seminar for the Pew Younger Scholars program, "Created Identities: Christianity and Literary Theory"—inspired me and listened to long digressions about "The Book."

Colleagues in the American Literature and Religion group—Roger Lundin, Laurence Buell, Harold Bush, Andrew Delbanco, James Dougherty, John Gatta, Barbara Packer, Gail MacDonald, Brian Ingraffia, Mark Walhout, and Ralph Wood—offered critique and support for parts of this work and general collegiality and inspiration. Albert Raboteau, Mark Noll, and John Stauffer, who joined us in Cambridge for a symposium, were also a great help in furthering my thinking on religion and literature. I owe a special thanks to Roger Lundin, of Wheaton College, for opportunities to share and publish my work in a variety of venues. Special thanks also to Ralph Wood, who laid the foundation for this building by piquing my interest in the intersection of religion and literature as a freshman at Wake Forest.

I also wish to thank the wonderful people at the University of Georgia Press—especially my editors, Erika Stevens and Melissa Buchanan—for all their help in bringing this project to completion.

I am among those blessed with a close, supportive spouse, family, and friend network. My life partner, Mark Bassard, and our two children, Angelique and Austin; my parents and parents-in-law; and a host of brothers, sisters-in-law, uncles, aunts, and friends—all have provided a secure net of safety and love within which the vision for this book has flourished. Thanks be to God for His indescribable gift!

TRANSFORMING SCRIPTURES

INTRODUCTION

the bible and african american women writers

A LITERARY WITNESS

Transforming Scriptures grew out of the research for my first book, *Spiritual Interrogations: Culture, Gender, and Community in Early African American Women's Writing*, as I was confronted with the range and depth of black women writers' references to the Bible in English.[1] From Phillis Wheatley to Toni Morrison, black women's literature is replete with biblical images, themes, and reverberations. This has been the case whether the Bible was being used to justify African enslavement or the second-class status of women, and continued even after texts had come under sharp hermeneutical and poststructural critique. While literary critics have long made mention of this fact, the subject has been handled anecdotally or in footnotes. This book is thus the first sustained treatment of the use of the Bible by African American women as an important feature of their literary self-representation. As my title *Transforming Scriptures* indicates, black women's historic encounters with the Bible were indeed transformational as they both reshaped and were shaped by the scriptures they appropriated. Their relationships to the Bible were dynamic and interactive rather than static, and they opened new possibilities for reimagining their place and position in society. In poetry, novels, speeches, sermons, and prayers, Maria W. Stewart, Frances E. W. Harper, Hannah Crafts, Harriet E. Wilson, and Harriet Jacobs from the nineteenth century, and later Zora Neale Hurston, Toni Morrison, and Sherley Anne Williams form a collective "literary witness" in response to the use of the Bible for purposes of social domination. *Transforming Scriptures* bears witness to their profound intellectual and theological engagements with the book Northrop Frye referred to as the "great code" of Western civilization.[2]

The subject of African Americans and the Bible is necessarily interdisciplinary, and I have drawn on work in religious studies (including biblical studies, black theology of liberation, and feminist/womanist theology), history, and hermeneutics, as well as literary criticism. Several studies on the Bible and African American culture inform my work and demonstrate the ongoing scholarly engagement with this topic, most notably Theophus Smith's *Conjuring Culture*, Vincent L. Wimbush's two edited volumes *African Americans and the Bible* and *Theorizing Scriptures*, Mark A. Noll's *America's God*, and Allen Dwight Callahan's *The Talking Book*. Robert Alter, Frank Kermode, Paul Ricoeur, and others have explored the subject of the Bible as literature but have paid almost no attention to race or gender in their work. Debora Shuger's *Renaissance Bible* bridges the gap between biblical exegesis and literary analysis, while works by Joycelyn Moody, Yolanda Pierce, and Cedric May have begun to correct the problem of the "invisibility" of religion in the study of literature.[3]

Two working premises form the basis of my analysis. First, African Americans were never a monolithic group of Bible readers but have, from their first encounters with the text, evidenced a range of Bible-reading practices. While writers from the Harlem Renaissance to the contemporary period, such as Zora Neale Hurston, Toni Morrison, and Sherley Ann Williams, proceed under sharp critiques of biblical authority and absolutes, women like Frances E. W. Harper, Maria Stewart, Hannah Crafts, Harriet E. Wilson, and Harriet Jacobs often blend cogent social critique with more traditional Protestant hermeneutics. Thus, African American women writers need to be located along a continuum of theological, textual, and political approaches to scripture.

Second, any assessment of the influence of the Bible on African Americans must take into account the Bible defense of slavery, the single most influential discourse on black Bible readers. As Callahan remarks in *The Talking Book*, "the Bible, as no other book, is the book of slavery's children" (xi). Moreover, a critique of the Bible defense of slavery occurs within a larger critical and hermeneutical climate that produced and supported the biblical justification of slavery and the textual grounds for refuting the proslavery ideologues. Thus, my approach for uncovering the multiple levels with which African American women writers engage the biblical text proceeds from overlapping theoretical concerns that are linguistic/textual, historical/ideological, and theoretical/hermeneutical.

I want to emphasize that my method here is deliberately and necessarily eclectic, since no single theoretical, critical, or hermeneutical approach is so all-encompassing as to apply equally to every instance of biblical intertextuality. As Theophus Smith suggests in his essay "'I Don't Read Such Small Stuff as Letters,'" the interaction between African Americans as a cultural/racial group and the Bible as a complex textual field is a problem of "intersubjectivities" involving biblical and nonbiblical, ethnic and nonethnic fields of analysis (88–90).

Each of the following chapters, then, is presented not as a part of an overarching schema or rubric but rather as an attempt to attend to more subtle undercurrents specific to the writers and texts under study. In this sense, this is not simply a historical study; while the majority of the writers are from the nineteenth century, I intentionally gesture toward twentieth-century and contemporary writers as fruitful subjects for further research.

The chapters of part 1, "Troubling Hermeneutics," are framed by the question, "What did African American women *see* in the Bible?" These are general theoretical and historical chapters that treat the emergence of the "curse" of blackness and womanhood in religious and social discourse and the "blessing" of black women's early formations of literary appropriations of scripture for their self-identity.

Chapter 1, "Talking Mules and Troubled Hermeneutics: Black Women's Biblical Self-Disclosures," traces black women's use of two important biblical figures around which they fashioned a counternarrative to the dominant culture's "curse" on black female identity. "The trope of the talking mule" comes from a reference in AME preacher Jarena Lee's 1849 *Religious Experience and Journal* to the story of the prophet Balaam and his donkey in the book of Numbers. As the story is told in Numbers 22–24, although Balaam is hired to curse Israel, he discovers he can only bless instead. "The trope of the talking mule" thus serves as a fitting representation of the emergence of black women's literary and intellectual discourse in the United States.

The most significant "curse" on black female identity was undoubtedly the slave law of *partus sequitur ventrem* (the law that mandated that the child shall follow the condition of the mother), which negated black female humanity and limited black women's sexuality to the passing on of chattel status to their offspring. The declaration of the Shulamite woman of Song of Songs—"I am black but comely" (Authorized Version)—marks the beginning of black women's reclamation of their subjectivity within a framework of desire and agency. Both of these tropes, then, demonstrate black women's rhetorical strategy of "turning cursing into blessing" as they appropriate the transformational impulse accorded to sacred texts within their own writings.

Chapter 2, "Private Interpretations: The Bible Defense of Slavery and Nineteenth-Century Racial Hermeneutics," traces the development of the Bible defense of slavery as a proslavery discourse in the first third of the nineteenth century and lays out, in broad strokes, a variety of African American responses to it from the radical revisionism of David Walker and Nat Turner to the milder revisionism of Frederick Douglass and Henry Bibb. Unlike their male contemporaries, who often participated in vigorous public debate, African American women writers tended to refute the Bible defense less in point-by-point debates and more in the field of literary representation. Therefore, I turn to the biblical poems of Frances E. W. Harper to show how she refutes the Bible defense within her representations of outsider biblical women and Jesus.

In part 2, "Transforming Scriptures," chapters 3 through 6 attempt to answer the question, "What did African American women writers *do* with the Bible?" In these chapters I consider how the nineteenth-century writers Maria W. Stewart, Hannah Crafts, and Harriet E. Wilson fashioned a variety of strategies of scriptural appropriation that challenge the Bible defense of slavery and the overall curse on their identity as sacred subjects. I also look at novels by two twentieth-century and contemporary writers—Sherley Anne Williams and Toni Morrison—to chart their extension and elaboration of the Shulamite trope for black female subjectivity.

Chapter 3, "Sampling the Scriptures: Maria W. Stewart and the Genre of Prayer," challenges earlier readings that reduce Stewart to only political and historical significance and marginalize or explain away her religious writings. In an examination of her religious meditations—which, literally, are placed centermost in her collections of essays and speeches—I locate these writings within the tradition of African American written prayers as a literary genre. Like her mentor David Walker in his *Appeal*, Stewart's meditations push the boundaries of written language to create multilayered, multivocal texts that "sample" the scriptures, pushing the genre of prayer to the level of cultural performance.

In chapter 4, "Hannah's Craft: Biblical Passing in *The Bondwoman's Narrative*," I propose to move beyond the debate over authorship and authenticity that has dominated Crafts's entry in the American/African American literary canons by focusing instead on her use of the biblical story of Esther, arguably the first passing narrative, and the figure of the Queen of Sheba in her own novel. By combining the passing narrative with the marriage plot, Hannah Crafts weaves a subtext into her narrative from which she deconstructs discourses of race, gender, and religion in nineteenth-century American culture.

Chapter 5, "'Beyond Mortal Vision': Identification and Miscegenation in the Joseph Cycle and Harriet E. Wilson's *Our Nig*," examines Wilson's use of the Joseph cycle, which ends the book of Genesis, as the vehicle for her own self-fashioning. The Joseph story becomes a literal and figurative mask for Wilson as she critiques the "American dream-text" of the "two story white house, North," by exposing the reality of northern racism and de facto slavery. Wilson situates the black woman writer as both teller and interpreter of dreams/texts.

Finally, chapter 6, "And the Greatest of These: *Eros*, *Philos*, and *Agape* in Two Contemporary Black Women's Novels," brings the analysis forward to the modern writers Toni Morrison and Sherley Anne Williams. For these writers, the Bible becomes the main locus for the formation of identity for African American women as they extend the Shulamite trope into representations of black women's ongoing struggle with empowered self-identity.

PART ONE

troubling hermeneutics

For now we see through a glass, darkly; but then face to face:
now I know in part; but then shall I know even as also I am known.
  1 Corinthians 13:12

What did African American women *see* in the Bible? How did they come to identify so strongly with an ancient, even foreign text?

While researching this topic, I was surprised to find a fourteenth-century woodcut from the *Speculum humanae salvationis* (*The mirror of man's salvation*), which depicted in a single panel two of the biblical tropes I identified as key to understanding the Bible in African American women's literature: the Balaam trope of the talking mule from Numbers 22, and the black but comely Shulamite from *Song of Songs*.[1] On the left side of this woodcut is an illustration of *Song of Songs* 4:12–15, replete with images of a walled garden, flowing fountain, and lush flora and vegetation, symbols said to prefigure the virginity of Mary. Facing right is an illustration from Numbers 22:24–34, the story of Balaam and his ass at the moment of confrontation with the Angel of the Lord. The reference to Balaam points to his prophecy of the birth of Jesus in a star, which is also thought to represent the Virgin Mary.

To readers unfamiliar with medieval allegory and typology—"the relating of the Old Testament to the life of Jesus Christ" (Wilson and Wilson 25)—these images seem oddly incoherent. Beyond the conspicuously absent Virgin, the feminine is completely missing from the visual field (in the illustration from the *Song of Songs*, there is not even a human figure). Important for this study, the voice of the Shulamite in *Song of Songs* who declares "I am black but comely" is also silenced, even as her blackness is erased. As we shall see, this disembodied black feminine poetics, or displaced black female body, of medieval allegory and typology reverberates through Western thought and biblical exegesis well into the nineteenth century.

For African American women, the historical context that has shaped their biblical self-fashionings is rooted in American chattel slavery and its biblical defense. Thus black women's reading of the Bible was not simply a matter of identification with certain scriptures or biblical characters; instead, they had to first read *through* a cultural discourse that had already "othered" them through American chattel slavery. The yoking together of a socially constructed racial and gendered inferiority with a text thought to be divinely sanctioned made Bible reading for African American women an ambivalent and potentially treacherous enterprise. They did not gaze into a mirror that reflected a clear, inviting image, but one already "darkened," to borrow St. Paul's phrase, with the Bible defense of slavery. Out of the "curse" of the social text of power in the nineteenth century, however, African American writers continually fashioned a "blessing" that turned the scriptures in a different direction.

> De nigger woman is de mule uh de world so far as Ah can see.
>
> ZORA NEALE HURSTON, *Their Eyes Were Watching God*

> I have heard that as far back as Adam Clarke's time, [an elder's] objections to female preaching were met by the answer—"If an ass reprove Balaam, and a barn-door fowl reprove Peter, why should not a woman reprove sin?" I do not introduce this for its complimentary classification of women with donkeys and fowls, but to give the reply of a poor woman, who had once been a slave. To the first companion she said—"May be a speaking woman is like an ass—but I can tell you one thing, the ass seen the angel when Balaam didn't."
>
> JARENA LEE, *Religious Experience and Journal*

> And when the ass saw the angel of the LORD, she fell down under Balaam: and Balaam's anger was kindled, and he smote the ass with a staff.
>
> And the LORD opened the mouth of the ass, and she said unto Balaam, What have I done unto thee, that thou hast smitten me these three times? . . . .
>
> Then the LORD opened the eyes of Balaam, and he saw the angel of the LORD standing in the way, and his sword drawn in his hand: and he bowed down his head, and fell flat on his face.
>
> NUMBERS 22:27–28, 31 (Authorized Version)

CHAPTER ONE

talking mules and troubled hermeneutics

BLACK WOMEN'S BIBLICAL SELF-DISCLOSURES

In Numbers 22–24 the Gentile prophet Balaam is hired by the Moabite King Balak to curse the ancient Israelites.[1] While he is supposedly gifted as a seer, Balaam's blindness is in contrast to the supernatural sight of the donkey who "saw the Angel of the Lord." A beast of burden, subjected to physical abuse, the donkey (or mule, or ass) is the ultimate image of powerlessness in the social hierarchy. Yet it is her supernatural vision and utterance that ensures Balaam's encounter with God, an encounter that will change the direction of the narrative. Only after Balaam listens to the donkey does the Lord open his eyes to the imposing sight of the Angel standing with the drawn sword (22:31). As we follow the story to its conclusion in Numbers 24, Balaam's encounter with God on the way to the plains of Moab, made possible through the speaking donkey, ensures that he will follow God's orders. Every time he thought to curse Israel, "the Lord put a word in Balaam's mouth" (23:5), and he could only pronounce blessings. As Alter and Kermode explain, "the divine will to bless is inalterable by human manipulation" (87).

The popularity of the Balaam story in the Middle Ages stemmed from its allegorical interpretation as prophesying the birth of Jesus in a star often figured as the Virgin Mary, as noted above. In other biblical references to Balaam, in both the Old and New Testaments, the prophet did not fare so well. In Numbers 31, for example, Balaam is blamed for leading the Israelites into idolatry and a troubling war of vengeance with Midian, during which "They also killed Balaam, son of Beor, with the sword" (31:8). In the New Testament book of Jude, he is characterized similarly as a villain and associated with treachery or betrayal.[2]

In the nineteenth and early twentieth centuries, references to the story of Balaam's ass took a variety of forms, from describing an actual mule, to representing unscrupulous ministers, to quoting Balaam's (misfired) prophetic discourse. Rev. Irving E. Lowery, in *Life on the Old Plantation in Ante-Bellum Days* (1911), imagined a mule named Ginnie speaking Shakespeare (34). In Joel Chandler Harris's folktale "Balaam and His Master," the slave is actually named Balaam, although ironically he functions in the story as the beast of burden, rather than as the biblical prophet. Joshua Lawrence in 1925 warned readers to beware "hirelings, Judases or Balaams" (*American Telescopes* 7). In a letter dated August 31, 1779, Ignatius Sancho admits to having misspoken, alluding to Numbers 23:8 when he writes, "like Balaam—I am constrained to bless where peradventure I intended the reverse" (79). Benjamin Tanner, in an 1867 *Apology for African Methodism*, compares the rapid increase in churches run by African Americans to the "tents of Israel" mentioned in Balaam's prophecy in Numbers 24:5.[3]

Often, however, we find the Balaam story of the talking ass used in racial discourse to refer to the phenomenon of educated or literate African Americans. In 1862, the story is completely misread by proslavery advocate T. W. MacMahon of Richmond, Virginia, in a scathing "review" of Harriet Beecher Stowe's *Uncle Tom's Cabin*. MacMahon derides Tom, stating that "the supernal ethics of Tom are ranked with the miraculous speeches of Balaam's ass. We do not mean to be skeptical, but simply critical" (*Cause and Contrast* 86). Although the talking mule is clearly the focus of the biblical version of the story, MacMahon, assuming Balaam represents white slave masters, sees him as the hero of the story: "were it not for the influence of the Angel and Balaam, it is equally doubtful, whether the Israelitish quadraped would have outstripped his brethren of the same species, and uttered prophecies of supernatural import" (86).

What is significant here is the interpretation of the Balaam story according to the racial dynamic of American chattel slavery. In an 1895 biography of Frederick Douglass titled *Frederick Douglass the Colored Orator*, which seems to be largely a summary of Douglass's autobiographical *Life and Times* (1881), Frederic May Holland quotes one of Douglass's speeches, in which he states, "It would have amazed the superior race as the ass's speech did Balaam. Now they mingle with applause in the debates with Garrison, and Foster, and Phillips" (64).

This context is helpful for distinguishing black women's unique interpretation and use of the Balaam story as a trope for their own agency and discourse. The passage quoted above from the *Religious Experience and Journal* (1849) of Jarena Lee, an AME itinerant preacher, references the nineteenth-century debate over women's right to preach, signified by the power to "take a text" from the Bible and interpret it. In introducing this passage from Numbers, Lee notes that she does not include this story "for its complimentary classification of women with donkeys and fowls, but to give the reply of a poor woman, who had once been a slave" (21). In opening a space in her text for the voice of one who had previously been silent, Lee stages the emergence of black women's voices through the formerly enslaved woman's sassy quip—"May be a speaking woman is like an ass—but I can tell you one thing, the ass seen the angel when

Balaam didn't." Not only has Lee, a licensed exhorter in the church, assumed the right to interpret the Bible, but she extends that right to the unnamed woman in her journal.[4]

For the woman (as for Jarena Lee), it was not the condition of the donkey as a beast of burden that was central to the story, but rather that it "seen the Angel." As William Andrews, Kimberly Rae Connor, Joycelyn Moody, and others have argued, this appeal to a special vision or insight is a key component of black women's spiritual narratives and serves as the foundation for later poets and novelists.[5] Indeed, nearly a century later, the trope of the talking mule was used in a familiar passage from Zora Neale Hurston's *Their Eyes Were Watching God* (1937). The metaphor of the mule resonates strongly with the story of Numbers 22, in which the donkey represents the socially disenfranchised, and I would not be surprised if Hurston, who was intimately familiar with the Bible, had this biblical story in mind.[6] Again, sight is the basis for Nanny's analysis of power relations of race and gender—"we don't know nothin' but what we see"—which she communicates to her granddaughter Janie, the novel's protagonist. Yet even within what appears to be an ironclad hierarchy of power, Nanny imagines "some place way off in de ocean" where things might be different. While these references to sight mark Nanny as a "seer" of social discourses of power, that her vision has limitations is intimated by the novel's title, which focuses on supernatural sight. Indeed, the novel traces the progression from Nanny's socially driven (in)sight to Janie's emergence as a seer with an alternative vision whose "eyes were watching God." The culmination, as in the Balaam story, is the translation of sight to voice as Janie's (re)telling of her story to Pheoby frames the novel.

In *The Souls of Black Folk*, W. E. B. DuBois theorized African American subjectivity as a function of the excess of vision produced by the othering gaze of white society: "the Negro is a sort of seventh son, born with a veil, and gifted with second-sight in this American world" (10). While the figure of the "veil" has negative connotations in DuBois's theory of "double-consciousness," it also positions the black subject as the "seventh son" (or daughter), last in the ubiquitous Types of Man anthropological system yet favored in biblical numerology and thus gifted with a kind of supernatural sight. The veil as caul thus positions African Americans as the seers or prophets of American race relations. Similarly, in the Hebrew Bible, the Prophet, always a marginal figure, is gifted with both supernatural sight and powerful, efficacious utterance as one who speaks what "thus saith the Lord."[7] David Lyle Jeffrey elaborates in *People of the Book*:

> It is essential to the character of a true Hebrew prophet that he himself has never sought the role. He is a *nabi'*—"one who is called." . . . The prophet has no prophetic training because none is necessary, and none is available. He is not a sorcerer, because he deals not so much with "secrets" or hidden things as with

that which has been revealed (cf. Deut. 29:28–30:3) He is not a shaman. He is simply and wondrously a mouthpiece, an amanuensis, a voice. (24–25)

Chanta M. Haywood makes the prophetic voice gender-specific in her essay "Prophesying Daughters." She defines the prophetic broadly as "the appropriation of a perceived mandate from God to articulate and spread God's word in order to advance a conscious or unconscious political agenda" (356). While Haywood's focus is solely on African American religious women of the nineteenth century, her definition is broad enough to have applicability to the writers in this study. As "voice[s] crying in the wilderness," black women's consistent turn to scripture for literary material is an attempt to position themselves as inheritors of the prophetic mantle.[8]

THE TURN: TRANSFORMING SCRIPTURES

> Nevertheless, the LORD thy God would not hearken unto Balaam;
> but the LORD thy God turned the curse into a blessing unto thee,
> because the LORD thy God loved thee.
> Deuteronomy 23:5 (Authorized Version)

Claus Westerman notes that the Balaam story in Numbers 22–24 represents the point in the narrative of the Hebrew Bible where "the originally nonhistorical or prehistorical concept of blessing is brought into union with history" (49). It is in this sense that I use the terms "cursing" and "blessing" as figures for the intersection of language, history, and agency within relations of social power. Thus, cursing and blessing refer to acts of language that are especially laden with social, historical, psychological, even spiritual, power and efficacy.[9] As Westerman continues, prophetic discourse, by its very nature, "presupposes the existence of gifted individuals who have the power to bless and to curse" (5). Moreover, the notion of blessing (and cursing) is "a generally known and widespread phenomenon of the history of religion where the spoken word is laden with power" (50). It is not, in such religious systems, simply that spoken words convey presence, but Presence in the sense of efficacious agency. The ability to *turn* (*hapak*—to turn, overturn, change, transform, turn back) cursing into blessing involves the redirecting of discourses of power in a way that is consistent with their original transformative potential.

The concept of biblical revisionism, or even signifying, does not account for the full range of strategies underlying black women's biblical intertextuality. In *The Talking Book*, Andrew Dwight Callahan proposes the dialectic between "the poison book" and "the good book" as a way of framing the discussion of African Americans and the Bible: "African Americans have held fast to the Bible only by holding fast to its contradictions" (25). Despite "toxic texts" that seem to uphold slavery and misogyny, "the Bible," Callahan writes, "had the power of curse and cure" (38). Because African Americans themselves "incarnated America's greatest contradiction" as slaves in a "free" land, Callahan suggests that blacks accepted and took in stride the contradictory nature of the Bible. "Ultimately," he concludes, "African Americans embraced the Bible, a poison book, because it was so effective, in measured doses, as its own antidote" (39).

Callahan's dialectical approach turns on a dichotomy of letter and spirit in keeping with the Pauline injunction, "the letter killeth but the spirit giveth life" (2 Corinthians 3:6). He writes: "Though African Americans early discerned a spirit of justice in the Bible, they discovered in the same moment that the letter of Holy Writ was sometimes at war with its spirit" (25). Callahan's dialectic accords loosely with what I refer to as "cursing" (poison book) and "blessing" (good book). My argument, however, is that rather than simply live with a set of contradictions, African American women writers invented an alternative hermeneutic that embodies both letter and spirit.

THE CURSE: POWER, LANGUAGE, AND BIBLICAL (MIS)REPRESENTATIONS

> Act XII. Children got by an Englishman upon a Negro woman shall be bond or free according to the condition of the mother, and if any Christian shall commit fornication with a Negro man or woman, he shall pay double the fines of the former act.
> Virginia State Law, 1662

Theophus Smith, in his interdisciplinary study *Conjuring Culture*, has argued persuasively that African Americans' contact with "the sacred text of western culture" must be viewed through an African sacred cosmos that prompted black American cultural adaptations of Euro-American Christianity. Thus, African American appropriations of biblical types and themes utilized the "western" Bible not as a theological treatise but as "a book of ritual prescriptions" for cultural formations of black American culture (3).

How the Bible—a compilation of dozens of texts written in the ancient Near East over a period of about two millennia—has come to be identified as *the* "Great Code" of Western European literary and cultural production is an interesting story in itself. Using Smith's definition of "conjuring culture" helps to illuminate ways in which Europeans have been "conjuring" with biblical material long before the first enslaved Africans arrived on these shores. Biblical scholar Cain Hope Felder puts it well in *Troubling Biblical Waters*: "whatever we may wish to say about the Bible, there is a need for a disciplined *skepticism* regarding its Western appropriations" (8, his emphasis). Specifically, the "Bible" that Euro-American enslavers presented to African Americans, read through western eyes, was already primed to enact and legitimate certain racial and gendered subjectivities of difference. I call this specific, historical conjuration with scriptures a curse (*qalal*), in the Hebrew sense of "making little or contemptible," since these interpretations served the purpose of social domination.

European "conjuring" with the Bible is especially evident with respect to the construction of racial ideology in early modern Europe. Indeed, the translation of the "Authorized Version," commonly referred to as the King James Version, was completed in 1611, well after the first English ships had begun transporting Africans from their homelands in 1572, and eleven years after Queen Elizabeth's proclamation in 1600 expelling all "blackamoores" from the country. As Robert Hood notes, "the Old Testament [Hebrew Bible] attaches no particular moral significance to the color black" (*Begrimed and Black* 105). Felder agrees: "*in antiquity, there existed no elaborate ideologies, theories, or definitions of race based on physical features and behavioral patterns*" (*Troubling Biblical Waters* 10, his emphasis). Yet the Genesis story of Noah's (not God's) cursing of Canaan (not Ham) was beginning to be interpreted as punishment of blackness in early Rabbinic writings and Christian scriptural commentary. In a Babylonian Talmud, for example, one rabbi claimed that "Ham was smitten in his skin" because of "copulating in the ark" (qtd. in Copher 147). Moreover, in *Midrash Rabbah Genesis* (midrash composed between the fourth and ninth centuries C.E.) we read that "Ham and the dog copulated in the Ark, therefore Ham came forth black-skinned" (qtd. in Copher 148). As one writer puts it, "no other verse in the Bible has been so distorted and so disastrously used down through the centuries for the exploitation of Africans and African Americans as Genesis 9:25" (Yamauchi 19). Oddly, one common thread in three major world religions of Judaism, Christianity, and Islam is this curious interpretation of the Ham/Canaan story. "In all three faiths," writes Hood, "Africa and its descendants were understood as the progeny of Ham who bear Noah's curse on Canaan, 'a slave of slaves shall he be to his brothers'" (155).[10]

Second only to the Hamitic curse in importance to European racial ideology was the interpretation based on the story of Cain (Genesis 4:1–16), the Bible's first murderer, upon whom God places a "mark"— presumably to spare his life from possible violent retaliation. Although the biblical story as we have it makes no racial claim (Cain and Abel, at this point in the narrative, are the only sons of the newly fallen Adam and Eve), "the mark of Cain" became associated with blackness, first in early rabbinic writings and then in European Christian discourse, at least as early as the twelfth century. In some cases, a black Cain has been linked to the Ham/Canaan story by having Ham marry a daughter of Cain, in an attempt to bridge the obvious continuity problem created by the supposed drowning of all of Cain's descendants in the intervening flood of Genesis 6. Perhaps the oddest of all these ideological constructions was the nineteenth-century "New Hamite" view that attempted to write African people out of the Bible altogether, declaring that "there is no black, especially Negro, presence in the Old Testament" (Copher 151).

In the case of African American women under slavery, upon whom a gendered subjectivity was simultaneously conferred and denied, the curse pronounced on Eve in the Garden is almost prophetic: "in sorrow shall you bring forth children." After the serpent's temptation and the eating of the fruit of the tree of the knowledge of good and evil, God pronounced a curse alternatively on the serpent, Eve, and Adam. This cursing of humanity is deeply gendered, since Adam's curse is in the area of production ("cursed is the ground for thy sake... thorns and thistles shall it bring forth to thee... in the sweat of thy face shalt thou eat bread" [Genesis 3:17–19]), while Eve's curse is in the area of reproduction and a restricted sexuality ("In sorrow thou shalt bring forth children; and thy desire shall be to thy husband and he shall rule over thee" [Genesis 3:16]). For enslaved African American women, the curse of reproduction goes beyond the physical pain of childbirth and is directly related to the economy of slavery, in which their *labor* is doubly inscribed; in this sense they bore the curse of Adam *and* Eve.

The idea of a double curse resonates with the theology of the "double fall" in racialized American religion, which was used to solve the central dilemma of the curse of Ham ideology—"if all the people descended from Adam and Eve and were therefore brothers and sisters, then how could whites enslave blacks, especially black Christians."[11] Thomas Smyth, a Presbyterian minister, put forth a theology whereby "Ham's 'original sin' caused his descendants to suffer under the yoke of slavery just as Eve's sin caused all women to suffer in childbirth and Adam's sin caused all humans to suffer from disease and death" (Hill 100). Thus, Ham and his African (American) descendants suffered a "double fall" from grace. Interestingly enough, the idea of the double fall was also applied to Jews in a conflation of racism and anti-Semitism.[12] When we remember the fact that black enslaved women bore the curses of both Adam *and* Eve, they can be described as suffering a *triple fall* as ideologies of difference morph into the law of *partus sequitur ventrem*—the decree that the child shall follow the condition of the mother. The schema for black women would look something like this:

Adam—original sin—death and disease (human)
Eve—childbirth (female)
Ham—slavery (black)

Of course while death, disease, and labor pains are all physical signs of the "curse," slavery is a man-made institution based upon the social construct of race.

The figures of Adam, Ham, and Eve collapse onto the enslaved black female body, marked within a prior narrative of illicit sexuality. (Recall that the blackness of Ham was sometimes attributed to unlawful copulation). Thus, African American women's sexuality becomes represented in legal discourse through the illicit—yet decriminalized—rape of black women by white men. The legal manifestation of the cursing of black womanhood appeared as the seventeenth-century Virginia law based on the Roman law of *partus sequitur ventrem*, in which the child follows the condition of the mother. The insidiousness of this intergenerational cursing was that it not only assigned to African American women a cursed or inferior legal status, but also demanded they pass on legal and social inferiority to their offspring. In the terminology of Orlando Patterson, black women became responsible for the "social death" of their children.[13] Thus African Americans' slave status became tied to the prior "fall" of black maternity. African Americans were, then, slaves for one reason and for one reason only: that they were of black women born.

Ironically, while the figure of the slave woman Hagar would seem a more natural representation of black womanhood in the nineteenth century, African Americans, male and female, are more often described as "children of Ham" or "sons [and daughters] of Ham." I suspect this is because of the perceived need to equate African Americans with the Hebraic line of the Old Testament, rather than with the non-Hebraic Gentile lineage. Hagar's Egyptianness would have been too dangerous to the pre-Emancipation cause of writing black Americans into the heroic narrative of Israelite deliverance and divine favor. Hagar will become more prominent in later black women's novels like Pauline Hopkins's serialized novel *Hagar's Daughter* (1901–2) and Toni Morrison's complex character Hagar in *Song of Solomon* (1977).

THE BLESSING: AFRICAN AMERICAN WOMEN WRITERS "OPEN" THE BIBLE

In her important early study *White Women's Christ, Black Women's Jesus*, theologian Jacqueline Grant noted that black people have "opened the Bible wider" than others; it is this ability to see beyond the types of ideological readings I've outlined above that leads to the prophetic act of "blessing" (*barak*) for self and community empowerment. Similarly, Elizabeth Schussler Fiorenza writes of the "doubly 'doubled' feminist strategy of suspicion and re-vision" (11) in her introduction to *Searching the Scriptures*. Fiorenza argues that the "hermeneutics of suspicion" of feminist Bible interpretation "invites readers to investigate biblical texts and traditions as one would 'search' the place and location where a crime has been committed. It approaches the canonical text as a 'cover-up' for patriarchal murder and oppression . . . in order to prevent further hurt and violations" (11). On the other hand, she notes, the "hermeneutics of re-vision . . . 'searches' texts for values and visions that can nurture those who live in subjection and authorize their struggles for liberation and transformation" (11).

In "Reading *Her Way* Through the Struggle," Hebrew Bible scholar Renita Weems notes a similar ambivalence in the reading practices of African Americans who "continue to view reading as an act clouded with mystery, power, and danger. The truth of this is evident in the ambivalence toward reading one can still detect within segments of the African American community—many still view reading as an activity that is at once commendable and ominous" (60). This ambivalence, argues Weems, extends to African American readings of the Bible, a text perceived as at once hostile and liberating. Womanist theologian Delores Williams, in her book *Sisters in the Wilderness*, underscores the gendered nature of this ambivalent reading practice by identifying a black male "*liberation tradition of African-American biblical appropriation*" (2, her emphasis) that focuses on an unproblematic identification with liberationist streams of biblical representation (e.g., the Exodus narrative). Williams contrasts this masculinist view with a "female-centered tradition" that she calls a "*survival/ quality-of-life tradition of African-American biblical appropriation*" (6). She argues that this female-centered reading practice, while sharing many of the liberationist practices of black male readers/theologians, embraces a more ambivalent appropriation strategy—one that is represented, for example, in black women's identification with a figure like the Egyptian slave Hagar in Genesis 16 and 21.

What I refer to as turning cursing into blessing argues for a way out of these dualisms through a hermeneutics of transformation that not only seeks to transform the dynamic between self and other but also preserves the transformational potential inherent in the notion of a sacred text. Thus the act of blessing must perform two actions at once: exposing the curse (*qalal*), the linguistic mechanism responsible for continuing structures of oppression, and redirecting the curse into the desired blessing.

Claus Westerman defines the ancient Hebraic concept of blessing (*barak*) as the power that "lets the soul grow and prosper so that it can maintain itself and do its work in the world." What is significant about the Hebrew concept of blessing (and by extension of cursing) is that it extends beyond the individual to the social and communal realms; it is, in Westerman's words, "both internal and external" (18). Derived from ancient understandings of the power of fertility (Genesis 1:22, 28), the meaning of *barak* unfolds in the patriarchal narratives of Genesis, and it is the main motif in the Abraham cycle of stories where "blessing is identified with the survival of the family" (18). It also extends to the power of "fruitfulness" (in the widest possible sense) and the power to defeat one's enemies.[14]

Westerman notes that the power of blessing has "'spiritual' as well as 'physical' effects" (19) and is related to the Wisdom tradition of the Hebrew Bible. Significantly, blessing and cursing as acts of language are interpersonal: "the act of blessing . . . means imparting a vital power to another person. The one who blesses gives the other person something of his own soul" (19). In ancient Hebrew culture, he writes, "interpersonal relations are not possible without blessing. When people meet, they bless each other" (19). In the New Testament, the concept of blessing extends to God's saving deeds in Christ (see Galatians 3:8–9, 14; Acts 3:25–26; Ephesians 1:3).[15]

Important for our study, Westerman goes on to elaborate on what he calls a "language of blessing," a semantic domain best summed up in the word *shalom*. Taken with *berakhah* (or *barak*), blessing then has a vertical (metaphorical) and horizontal (metonymic) axis: *berakhah* is "the power of growth vertically, from generation to generation," while *shalom* represents "the well-being of a community horizontally" (29).

There are three types of blessing in the Hebrew Bible:

Patriarchal Blessing—intergenerational (Genesis 49ff.), speaking words of blessing from one generation to another

Priestly Blessing—intercessory (e.g., Moses), where the blesser stands as the mediator between God and people, divine and human

Prophetic Blessing—interventional (e.g., Balaam, Hebrew Prophets) blessing that directs a divine warning to the hearers and contains the power to bring into being the words spoken

Using this rubric, we could outline a similar understanding of black women's biblical transformations:

Matriarchal—tropes, such as the talking mule and the Shulamite, that work across generations of black women to designate an historical writing community (e.g., Jarena Lee and Zora Neale Hurston; Zilpha Elaw, Hannah Crafts, and, later, Sherley Anne Williams and Toni Morrison)

Priestly—utterance that foregrounds black women's texts as interpretive and intercessory (e.g., Maria W. Stewart and Harriet E. Wilson)

Prophetic—contestation over meanings and definitions of power and narrative that are interventional (e.g., Sherley Anne Williams and Toni Morrison)

These categories are not mutually exclusive, and, as we shall see, elements of all three—matriarchal/intergenerational, priestly/intercessory, and prophetic/interventional—are present in the writers examined in this study.

BLACK *AND* COMELY: THE SHULAMITE TROPE IN AFRICAN AMERICAN WOMEN'S WRITING

> For the signifier, by its very nature, always anticipates meaning by unfolding its dimension before it. As is seen at the level of the sentence when it is interrupted before the significant term.... Such sentences are not without meaning, a meaning all the more oppressive in that it is content to make us wait for it.
> But the phenomenon is no different which by the mere recoil of a "But" brings to light, comely as the Shulamite, honest as the dew, the negress adorned for the wedding and the poor woman ready for the auction block.
>
> Jacques Lacan, "The Agency of the Letter in the Unconscious"

As we have seen, starting from the Middle Ages the figure of Balaam is often yoked to representations of the *Song of Solomon*. The book known in the Old Testament as *Song of Solomon*, *Song of Songs*, or *Shir Hashirim*, is a love song divided into eight chapters in English translations and usually, though not always, rendered in poetic lines of text.[16] It is part of the Wisdom literature in the Hebrew Bible, the tradition Westerman associates most closely with *barak*. The poem progresses through a series of voices in dialogue, interspersed with a chorus of female voices referred to as "the daughters of Jerusalem" (1:5, 2:7, 3:5, 5:16). Like the Hebrew notion of *barak*, communal and interpersonal language is thus a major feature of the *Song*.

Dubbed "the least 'biblical' of all the biblical books" (LaCocque 262), *The Song of Songs* has generated millennia of interpretive history, starting from the patristic age to the Latin and late Middle Ages.[17] Most of the contention over interpretations of the *Song* centers on the predominance of allegory as the chief hermeneutical basis for its biblical significance and, perhaps, its inclusion in the canon of scriptures in the first place. The lovers are thought to stand for, alternatively, Israel and God, or the Church and Christ, depending on the religious tradition at hand. As E. Ann Matter states, "there is no 'non-allegorical' Latin tradition of *Song of Songs* commentary," and indeed the body of commentary "tell[s] a story of the triumph of the allegorical" in the Middle Ages (4). In *The Voice of My Beloved*, she reads the *Song of Songs* as a "metacritical genre" of biblical poetry that "provides an important key to other literary forms" (11). This concept of a "key" that unlocks a code (itself a metaphor for allegory) is echoed in other writers on the *Song* as literature. For example, Julia Kristeva describes the *Song* as "a chest whose keys have been lost" ("A Holy Madness" 86).

This discussion of the metacritics of the *Song* demonstrates the hermeneutical dance of its representations of gender, racial difference, and sexuality, which opens up a space for alternative readings that turn cursing—"black but comely"—into blessing—"black and beautiful." Paul Ricoeur's delineation of the interpretive history of the *Song* into four distinct epochs, culminating in what he calls the "almost universal triumph of erotic reading" (*Thinking Biblically* 294), offers a way of theorizing black women's move away from allegory toward more narrative interpretive strategies.[18] In the case of this biblical love poem, black women's use of the Shulamite trope is not simply a matter of choosing between competing allegorical interpretations. As Andre LaCocque states, in *Song of Songs* "language has come full circle, from literal sense to metaphorical to non-figurative again" (251). It is this play between literal and metaphorical that black women writers exploit in their nineteenth-century and contemporary readings and rewritings of the *Song*.

Jacques Lacan's description of the process of signification in "The Agency of the Letter in the Unconscious" contains a casual allusion to the "comely... Shulamite" of the biblical *Song of Songs*, which accepts uncritically an already racially inflected mistranslation of 1:5 rendered in the Authorized Version as "I am black *but* comely" (my emphasis). The rendering of the conjunction "but" instead of "and" (an equally plausible translation) has had powerful consequences for the lives of women of color, especially women of African descent. In this one verse we encounter many of the hermeneutical problems and possibilities that attend African American, feminist, and "othered" readings of the Bible.

Significantly, the Septuagint—the Greek translation of the Hebrew Bible completed ca. 200 B.C.E., and the scriptures at the time of Jesus—translated the verse "I am black *and* beautiful" (my emphasis). Centuries later the Latin Vulgate translator Jerome rendered the verse "I am black *but* comely," and the Authorized Version followed the Vulgate. Several modern translations—including the New International Version (NIV), the New King James Version (NKJV), the New American Standard Bible (NASB)—all translated the conjunction "yet"; the Living Bible "but beautiful"; and the New Revised Standard Version (NRSV) "and." Interestingly enough, the *African American Heritage Bible* uses the AV rendering but adds a headnote that reads: "I am black and beautiful."

In interpretations by the early church fathers, the verse did not have racial significance. Origen read the Shulamite allegorically as a figure for the Gentile church and associated blackness with Christ. Luther felt that the "but" refers to the contrast between the tents of Kedar and the tents of the courts referenced in the *Song*. While these early interpretations did not read the conjunction in connection with racial discourse, it later became part of discourses that posited European standards of beauty as normative. In this sense, African American women's subjectivity and discourse are located precisely between the "but/and" configuration represented by the history of translation and interpretation of this verse. A black feminist epistemology is precisely an epistemology of the "but"—simultaneously reading and critiquing the ways in which black women have been constructed as other and revising the terms of that construction in language.

Like the Balaam trope of the talking mule, the Shulamite's words—"black but comely"—figured in a range of nineteenth-century racial discourses, including African American women writers' appropriations of the Scriptures for their self-representations. Although the phrase is clearly gendered in the biblical passage, it was often used to describe African American men. John Jea, the black, ex-slave preacher, wrote:

> Frequently did they tell us we were made by, and like the devil, and commonly called us black devils; not considering what the Scriptures saith in the Songs [sic] of Solomon, "I am black but comely. Look not upon me, because I am black, because the sun hath looked upon me my mother's children were angry with me; they made me keeper of the vineyards; but mine own vineyard have I not kept." This latter sentence was verified in the case of us poor slaves, for our master would make us work, and neglect the concerns of our souls. (*Life, History and Unparalleled Suffering of John Jea*, 9)

In his black male autobiography, Jea uses the phrase to apply, presumably, to enslaved blacks as a whole as a way of refuting the white racist conception of Africans as "black devils." By the end of the passage, however, "black but comely" becomes equated with neglected "souls" in a shift from outward description to inner (spiritual) condition.

Similarly, in 1853 Frederick Douglass used the Shulamite's words to describe his fictional character Madison Washington in his novella *The Heroic Slave*: "Madison was of manly form. Tall, symmetrical, round, and strong. In his movements he seemed to combine, with the strength of the lion, a lion's elasticity. His torn sleeves disclosed arms like polished iron. His face was 'black, but comely'" (179). The appropriation of the phrase to represent heroic black manhood was continued by Archibald H. Grimke in his 1901 book about Denmark Vesey, titled *Right on the Scaffold, of The Martyrs of 1822*, and applied to the description of Vesey himself: "He was black but comely. Nature gave him a royal body, noble planned and proportioned, and noted for its great strength" (3). Just two years later, W. E. B. DuBois included the passage from *Song of Songs* 1:5 as the epigraph to his essay "Of the Black Belt" in his *Souls of Black Folk* (174).

For African American women, the phrase had a double resonance of racial and gendered meanings. Zilpha Elaw grasped the significance of the translation issue in the dedication to her 1846 edition of her spiritual autobiography, *Memoirs of the Life, Religious Experience, Ministerial Travels and Labours of Mrs. Zilpha Elaw, An American Female of Color*. Writing to her Methodist friends "in London and other localities in England" on the eve of her return to the United

States, she remarks:

> I feel that I cannot present you with a more appropriate keepsake, or a more lively memento of my Christian esteem, and affectionate desires for your progressive prosperity and perfection in Christian calling, than in the following contour portrait of my regenerated constitution—exhibiting, as did the bride of Solomon, comeliness with blackness; and, as did the apostle Paul, riches with poverty, and power in weakness—a representation, not, indeed, of the features of my outward person, drawn and coloured by the skill of the penciling artist, but of the lineaments of my inward man, as inscribed by the Holy Ghost, and, according to my poor ability, copied off for your edification. (51)

Elaw's subtle rewriting of *Song of Songs* 1:5 through her phrase "comeliness *with* blackness" (my emphasis) overturns the racial pejorative of the original terms. It could be argued that her insistence on the conjunction "with" simply emphasizes the customary translation of "but"; however, in fact it represents Elaw's awareness of the larger issue of the use of biblical language as a vehicle for self-expression. Seen in this light, she could be said to anticipate and challenge Lacan's theory of oppressive signification in "The Agency of the Letter in the Unconscious" by troping both the Shulamite woman he references and the "poor woman on the auction block," redirecting the axes of power and agency. The conjunction "but" in both "black but comely" and "poor but honest" is oppressive only if one sees no way around the expectation and assumption signaled by the linguistic act. Yet Elaw, in changing both "buts" to "with" (or "and") simply refuses the terms of her own disempowerment.

Chapter six will explore the extension of this trope for the contemporary women writers Sherley Anne Williams and Toni Morrison. First, however, I will turn to the context within which black women's self-representation is embedded, namely, the Bible defense of slavery and the response to this discourse in the poetry of Frances E. W. Harper.

"I think de people dat made de Bible was great fools," said Ned.

"Why?" Uncle Simon.

"'Cause dey made such a great big book and put nuttin' in it, but servants obey yer masters."

WILLIAM WELLS BROWN, *Clotel* (1853)

CHAPTER TWO

private interpretations

THE BIBLE DEFENSE OF SLAVERY AND
NINETEENTH-CENTURY RACIAL HERMENEUTICS

For much of its life in America, the Bible was not conceived of as just a "good *book*" but as the "*Good* Book," as scripture and therefore vested with sacred authority and divine intentionality. In his introduction to *Theorizing Scriptures*, Vincent Wimbush proposes a reconsideration of the term *scripture* that places the primary focus "*not upon texts* per se (that is, upon their content meanings), but upon textures, gestures, and power—namely the signs, material products, ritual practices and performances, expressivities, orientations, ethics and politics associated with the phenomenon of the invention and use of 'scriptures'" (3). Wimbush thus advocates an approach to scripture that involves "naming loudly (or critically analyzing) the nature and consequences of interpretive practices, their strategies, and play, especially in terms of power relations" (5). It is in this spirit that I began an exploration of the proslavery Bible defense, in order to uncover the hermeneutic principles that underwrote its claims.

The question of what constitutes scripture is the necessary starting point, as Wimbush suggests. In the postscript to *An American Bible*, Paul Gutjahr takes a "history of the book" approach to defining scripture, suggesting that attention to material textual history forces us to reconsider the Protestant notion of *sola scriptura*. For Gutjahr, the "scripturalness" of the Protestant Bible is both reflected in, and in turn constituted by, certain material markers of difference—leather binding, size, elaborate illustration, and so forth.

Stephen J. Stein connects the concept of scripture with definitions and delineations of readerly communities and draws attention to three "canons within the canon" that are important for my analysis here:

> Three different scriptures—Jefferson's personal bible, the African American conjurational canon, and *The Woman's Bible*—are each *defined by a particular religious, social, or political agenda of an interactive community*. The mode of

> expression in each varies—a private document, oral performances by singers and preachers, and a political manifesto. Yet in each case the essential elements of the scripturalizing process are present—canon, commentary, and community. ("America's Bibles," 182, my emphasis)

Using Theophus Smith's term of an African American "conjurational canon," Stein collapses all African American hermeneutics into one framework, as if a "black Bible" exists that derives from a unitary individual consciousness, like Jefferson's or Stanton's. However, from their earliest contact with the Christian Bible, African American readers exhibited a range of approaches to biblical material and the question of the Bible's authority, from orthodox Christian readings to radical revisionist appropriations. It is helpful, therefore, to frame our discussion of nineteenth-century African American biblical interpretation(s) by exploring the two documents known as Jefferson's "Bible" (*The Philosophy of Jesus* [1804] and *The Life and Morals of Jesus of Nazareth* [1819–20]) from the beginning of the nineteenth century and Stanton's *Woman's Bible* (1895) from the century's end.¹

Jefferson's extracts from the Gospels did not come to public attention until the mid-nineteenth century—the period when, according to Gutjahr, Bible publishing was at its peak. Jefferson's belief in a purely privatized religion made him reluctant to speak publicly about his own religious views. While Jefferson's views were personal, they were far from purely private, shaped, as they were, by Enlightenment demands for rationality and utility in religious institutions. Thus, ironically, Jefferson's very private biblical readings were shaped by larger public debates about rationalism and biblical accuracy posed by the German Higher Criticism, which began to infiltrate American religion via liberal movements like Unitarianism. By all accounts, Jefferson experienced a "religious crisis" during the 1760s, stumbling over the doctrine of the Trinity, which he could not reconcile with the Bible's insistence on monotheism. Out of that crisis, Jefferson began in the 1760s and 1770s to piece together a "commonplace book consisting of extracts from the writings of various ancient and modern dramatists, philosophers, poets," a "literary Bible" (Adams 11). Important for my purposes here, Jefferson's highly privatized, even secretive, "commonplace book" stemmed from his demand for reason and utility in religious institutions and texts. In fact, so skeptical was Jefferson about the historicity of the Bible's account of Creation that he became an early speculator of the theory of polygenesis, the "'suggestion' that blacks might have been originally created as a distinct race" (Adams 11). Like his Unitarian counterparts, Jefferson held to a "demystified" and "demythologized" form of Christianity.

Unlike Jefferson's "Bible," which was a work precipitated by a youthful spiritual crisis, Elizabeth Cady Stanton's *Woman's Bible* was written soon after her eightieth birthday following a radical shift in her views about organized religion and scriptures. Earlier, Stanton had echoed the "positive, reform-minded biblical interpretation" of other women's rights activists like Sarah Grimke and Lucretia Coffin Mott, but her view changed radically in the 1880s and 1890s. In "rejecting the Bible as the Word of God," and "defin[ing] the Bible as the foundation of women's oppression and the greatest stumbling block to women's complete emancipation" (Strange 374), Stanton anchored her biblical commentary in the intellectual discourses of the nineteenth century that flowed from the Enlightenment: "wholesale attack on organized religion" led Stanton to call for "*a more 'rational' religion, much like such eighteenth-century Deists as Thomas Jefferson and Thomas Paine*. Unlike the Deists, however, Stanton's theological revisionism aimed primarily to empower women" (Strange 374, my emphasis). The relation of Stanton's feminism to the rationalism of Jefferson and Paine points to the fact that there are wider social issues informing Stanton's biblical revisionism than allegiance to women's community or political activism, as Stein's community-based hermeneutics would maintain.[2] Indeed the invocation of Jefferson and Paine traces an ideological and interpretive legacy that has at its core the issue of the decentering of biblical authority and contestations over new sources of authority for meaning and texts. As Kathi Kern points out, *The Woman's Bible* was, more particularly, "Mrs. Stanton's Bible."[3]

In *"Take, Read": Scripture, Textuality and Cultural Practice*, Wesley A. Kort argues for the retention of the category of "scripture" as both textual and cultural practice. For Kort, such a category needs to be "recovered and reconstructed" because of the breakdown in premodern notions of the Bible as scripture (as opposed to literature or history). Thus, scripture "functions as a category in textural and cultural theory to designate the locations of persons, groups, and institutions on the textual field" (3). In other words, scripture is not simply the constitution of texts as such, due to materiality of form and distribution, as Gutjahr proposes, nor is it community consensus, as Stein maintains; instead, "scriptures" exist as primary locations of identities. Scripture is, moreover, "a textual designation that stands somewhere between 'writing,' with its suggestion of nonspecificity and dislocation, and 'canon,' with its suggestion of autonomy and transcendence."[4] As a median category of analysis or reading strategy, then, scripture allows us to map the locations and displacements of various identities in and through a given textual field.

I take the term "private interpretations" from the Authorized Version of the New Testament epistle of 2 Peter 1:20–21: "knowing this first, that no prophecy of the scripture is of any private interpretation. For the prophecy came not in old time by the will of man: but holy men of God spake as they were moved by the Holy Ghost." What interests me in these verses are the Greek words that are translated "private" and "interpretation," which stem from the word *idios* (or "individual") and the verb *luo* ("to loose," in the sense of an unraveling, or an "undoing" that is more akin to our poststructuralist terminology of "dismantling").⁵ This private interpretation, or "individual loosening" of the text, as demonstrated by both Jefferson and Stanton in different eras and for different purposes, involves a two-step process: first, a selection of certain passages around a common theme (moral philosophy or gender, in this case), which effects a "shrinking" of the canon and virtual "recanonization." Second (and in a related fashion), the addition of commentary (in Jefferson's case, the presence of other, nonbiblical materials and literature) effects a "recontextualization" of the material. Thus, the private interpreter first shrinks the Bible to a select number of passages, then proceeds to comment on those as though they served as a representation of the whole text. Moreover, upon close examination, this process always reveals an allegiance to a prior "scripture" that authorizes the privatized reading, even if the interpreter purports to appeal to no other authority than the Bible itself. As we will see, this is exactly the methodology of proslavery advocates. It may be even more surprising that African Americans, seeking to build a counter-hermeneutic, often employed their own "private interpretations" as well. Finally, I will turn briefly to the poetry of Frances E. W. Harper as she mounts a poetic challenge to the Bible defense of slavery.

THE RISE (AND DOWNFALL) OF THE BIBLE DEFENSE OF SLAVERY

In his article "New Testament Interpretation in Historical Perspective," Anthony C. Thiselton calls for an "emancipatory hermeneutics as neither a pull toward nor a flight from history as such, but as a call to renounce manipulative interpretation of all kinds" (36). When one thinks of nineteenth-century America, one would be hard-pressed to find a better example of "manipulative" hermeneutics than within the debate over American slavery as such debate centered on appeal to biblical authority. While it is axiomatic that proslavery forces used the Bible to justify the enslavement of African/African American people, the question of what type of hermeneutical assumptions or theory of textuality authorized such racially oppressive use of scripture has been understudied.⁶ I find it interesting, for example, that in a variety of cultural historical, theological, and literary accounts of the nineteenth century, one repeatedly finds a link between proslavery exegesis and "literalism"—understood to mean a surface-level, face-value reading of the Bible—as opposed to an antislavery or natural rights ideology and a "freer" reading of the Bible that ventures off from a simplistic, literal reading. Moreover, by "literal" reading, scholars always imply a simple faith in the authority of scripture.

Mark Noll's compelling account of the debate over the Bible and slavery in *America's God* comes closest to dealing with the hermeneutical issue behind the controversy that he calls "a theological crisis of the first order" (387). He bases his argument on the idea that the "formidable" arsenal of the proslavery argument depends on the "reformed and literal hermeneutic." As Noll points out, quoting Lincoln, not only were both North and South "read[ing] the same Bible," but "both were reading Scripture in just about the same way" (386). According to Noll, this left three options for dealing with the dilemma of the Bible and slavery:

1. Liberation versus the Bible—"to admit that the Bible sanctioned slavery and therefore to abandon the Bible" altogether (387). This was the route taken by radical abolitionists like William Lloyd Garrison, who, influenced by his reading of Thomas Paine, proposed being guided by "the province of reason" when interpreting scripture.
2. The Bible in Defense of Slavery—"the stance of most Southern theologians and a large number of their Northern colleagues" (388). Not only did this viewpoint cross regional boundaries, but the accessibility of its commonsense approach meant that "any thoughtful believer who could find the word 'slavery' in a biblical concordance was a potential convert to this view" (388).
3. Mediating Positions—in this category Noll places the infamous split between "letter" and "spirit" that characterizes much antislavery discourse: "it conceded that, while the Bible did indeed sanction a form of slavery, careful attention to the text of Scripture would show that the simple presence of slavery in the Bible was not a necessary justification for slavery as it existed in the United States" (389–90). Thus, these moderate abolitionists "distinguish[ed] between the letter of the Bible (which might be construed to allow slavery) and the spirit of the Bible (which everywhere worked against the institution)" (390).

The difficulty with the mediating position was that, in conceding some of the exegetical ground to proslavery advocates, moderate abolitionists actually "*shifted the ground on which interpretation took place*" (Noll 391, my emphasis). Thus, antislavery advocates who wished to use the Bible as their source of authority "faced a double burden of staggering dimensions":

> Any who wished to make such arguments first had to execute the delicate intellectual task of showing that literal proslavery interpretations did not adequately exegete the apparently straightforward biblical texts. Then they were compelled to perform an intellectual high-wire act by demonstrating why arguments against slavery should not be regarded as infidel attacks on the authority of the Bible itself. (390)

This linking of authoritative biblicism with slavery and decentered biblical authority with liberation has shaped much biblical scholarship.

It is here that the understanding of scripture as a textual issue, an issue of language, helps to reframe the debate over the Bible and slavery. Wesley Kort traces a progression from an understanding of the Bible as scripture—and thus as the authoritative source of meaning—in the sixteenth century by a writer like Calvin, to the notion of nature, history, and finally literature as scripture in the nineteenth and twentieth centuries. Finally he locates in postmodernity the dismantling of the category of scripture altogether. Intertwined with this exchange of centers of authority and authority structures is a secondary process in which the extrabiblical "scripture" (nature, history, and literature, respectively) is first understood as warranted by the Bible, then as competing with and finally as supplanting the Bible. In an almost ironic twist, the new "scripture," originally justified as biblically mandated, becomes now the ground of authority from which the Bible must be read. Interpretations of the Bible, therefore, must give account to the new "scripture," now viewed as the authority of not only biblical meaning but meaning itself.[7]

In "Everyone One's Own Interpreter? The Bible, Science, and Authority in Mid-Nineteenth-Century America," George Marsden notes a similar complicity between Enlightenment ideology and biblical textuality: as Enlightenment. Dubbed the "common sense" approach, such a hermeneutic depended on the belief that "the God of science was after all the God of Scripture. It should not be difficult to demonstrate, therefore, that what he revealed in one realm perfectly harmonized with what he revealed in the other. The perspicuity of nature should confirm the perspicuity of scripture" (86). I suggest that this belief in the harmony of scripture and nature is behind the use of scripture in the debate over the enslavement of Africans in America that comes to a peak in the nineteenth century, a debate of great interest to African Americans, and one that has profoundly shaped African American readings of the Bible and the subsequent use of the Bible in their writings. Moreover, when we examine these debates in light of textuality and hermeneutical practice, it becomes clear that the prevailing understanding of the "nature of the Negro" as inherently and biologically inferior to whites constitutes the real ground of authority for proslavery readings of the Bible. Thus, proslavery advocates often did not derive their belief in black inferiority *from* the Bible, as they claimed, but from empirical "evidences" of science and experience. Standing on the high ground of experience, "common sense" reasoning, and often developments within natural science and natural philosophy, the proslavery camp invented a hermeneutic that shackled the biblical text in either a hyperliteralistic or, as often, a fancifully allegorical recontextualization. What is missing between these two poles, however, is the possibility of a literal reading that carries with it the assumption of biblical authority and historicity and provides the ground for a black/antislavery emancipatory hermeneutic practice.[8]

Slaveholders' commitment to a prior "scripture" of black racial inferiority ultimately contributed to the dismantling of the authority of the very Bible upon which they claimed to stand. Indeed, it could be argued that the turn to scientific racism in the 1850s was necessitated, at least in part, by the fact that the proslavery biblical argument helped to undermine the appeal to biblical authority and contributed to the rise of science as the new ground of authority.

It is through the development and dissemination of the proslavery hermeneutic that we locate African Americans within the textual field of racial "scriptures" in the nineteenth century. As Mark Noll remarks in *America's God*, the debate over the Bible and slavery "was more than an exegetical debate. . . . [I]t was always a question of who had the power to dictate how the Bible should be interpreted and who had no voice in shaping the accepted canons of interpretation. The issue from first to last was an issue of cultural hermeneutics as well as biblical exegesis" (395).

In William Sumner Jenkins's early account of proslavery thought, the authority of the biblical text was often secondary to the allegiance to a prior discourse of racial inferiority. Jenkins traces proslavery thought from its beginnings in 1701 with John Saffin's *A Brief and Candid Answer to a Late Printed Sheet, Entitled The Selling of Joseph* through its engagement with natural rights philosophy during the American Revolution and then to the moral philosophy and ethnological debates in the mid-nineteenth century, right up until the Civil War. Noting that proslavery thought is "characteristically defensive in nature" (39), Jenkins observes that in its early incarnations, proslavery thought "denied general principles of natural equality of men and argued that divine revelation showed inequality to be the natural order of the universe" (39). Yet throughout the first third of the eighteenth century, Jenkins notes, "the slaveholder relied upon the historical sanction, that slavery was a natural phenomenon of society, which had existed in all ages" (40). It is from this historical sanction of slavery as "natural," I contend, that slaveholders derived "the Biblical sanction" for African enslavement.

The assumption of a normative whiteness led to a feverish rush to account for the blackness of African skin color beginning in the age of exploration. In his definitive study *White Over Black*, Winthrop D. Jordan writes that the range of possible answers to account for the blackness of Africans was "rigidly restricted . . . by the virtually universal assumption, dictated by church and Scripture, that all mankind stemmed from a single source" (12). This "universalist strain" (22) in Christian thought militated against an overdetermined doctrine of essential difference, while maintaining theological categories of "Christian" and "heathen" as categories of distinction. Jordan argues that explorations into biblical conceptualizations of blackness arose from "a feeling that blackness could scarcely be anything *but* a curse and by the common need to confirm the facts of nature by specific reference to Scripture" (19). By the seventeenth century, these "facts of nature" (the "feeling" that black skin color constituted a "curse") had become a competing discourse, a "scripture," if you will, that would ultimately, two centuries later, supplant the Bible and hold it accountable to this new discourse. Thus a specifically racialized hermeneutic developed for the express purpose of the oppression and exploitation of peoples of African descent. If the "Book of Nature" came to compete with the "Book of Books" as the center for authority and meaning, the text of color difference constituted at least a chapter that marked Africans and their descendants as inherently and naturally inferior. The belief in African inferiority as evidenced by black skin color became so widespread an assumption as to constitute a kind of subconscious marginalia in the reading of the Bible itself.

As Jordan writes of the attempts to use the so-called curse of Ham text of Genesis 9, "the difficulty with the story of Ham's indiscretion was that extraordinarily strenuous exegesis was required in order to bring to bear on the Negro's black skin" (19). This "extraordinarily strenuous exegesis," I might add, operated in two directions: extremely literalistic (as opposed to literal) and allegorical.[9] The Bible anticipates both exegetical extremes in the Book of Revelation 22:18–19:

> For I testify unto every man that heareth the words of the prophecy of this book, If any man shall add unto these things, God shall add unto him the plagues that are written in this book: And if any man shall take away from the words of the book of this prophecy, God shall take away his part out of the book of life, and out of the holy city, and from the things which are written in this book. (AV)

What I would call allegorical readings could be loosely called "adding to" scripture, that is, supplying a context that is extrabiblical. What I call literalistic would be "taking away from," which is clearly ignoring the historical, literary, rhetorical, and linguistic contexts of the biblical passage. Kevin J. VanHoozer describes a literalistic reading as "one that insisted on staying on the level of ordinary usage, even when another level is intended" (117). Thus it is that the "literalistic reading is less than fully 'literal'—that is insufficiently and only thinly literal" (311):

> It is most important to distinguish literalistic from literal interpretation. The former generates an unlettered, ultimately *illiterate* reading—one that is incapable of recognizing less obvious uses of language such as metaphor, satire, and so forth.... Literal interpretation, on the other hand, is more like a translation that strives for dynamic equivalence and *yields the literary sense*. The distinction, then, is between "empirically minded" interpreters, who, in their zeal for factual correspondence, take an unimaginative, almost positivist, view of things, and "literate-

minded" readers, who are sensitive to context and familiar with how literary texts work. (311, my emphasis)

VanHoozer also maintains a distinction between the literal, the literalistic, and the allegorical when he notes that "interpreters err either when they allegorize discourse that is intended to be taken literally or when they 'literalize' discourse that is intended to be taken figuratively" (311).

A literalistic reading, for example, occurred in a pamphlet by Alexander McCaine, *Slavery Defended from Scripture, Against the Attacks of the Abolitionists in the Methodist Protestant Church in Baltimore 1842*. Writing of Noah's drunken proclamation, "Cursed be Canaan; a slave of slaves shall he be to his brothers [Shem and Japheth]" (Genesis 9:25), McCaine asserts that Noah "spoke under the impulse and diction of Heaven. His words were the words of God himself, and by them was slavery ordained. This was an early arrangement of the Almighty, to be perpetuated through all time" (qtd. in H. Shelton Smith, *In His Image*, 130). McCaine clearly reads past the mediation of Noah as the protagonist of the narrative, a practice that popular Bible commentators such as Adam Clarke, a favorite cited authority of slaveholders, helped set in motion.[10] On the text of Genesis 9:22–24, for example, Clarke writes: "Had Noah not been innocent, as my exposition supposes him, God would not have endued him with the spirit of prophecy on this occasion, and testified such marked disapprobation of their conduct. . . . On the one hand the spirit of prophecy (not the incensed father) pronounces a curse: on the other the same spirit (not parental tenderness) pronounces a blessing" (130). This attribution to Noah of "prophetic" ("thus saith the Lord") speech emanates not from the text but from Clarke's "supposition" about Noah's innocence. Upon the reading of Noah's speech as unmediated divine discourse, then, depends the "cursing" of Ham's/Canaan's (read Africa's) progeny and the "blessing" of Japheth's (Europe's) descendants. This "curse," according to Jenkins, was "the ultimate basis on which the religious element in the South justified slavery" (204). As abolitionist Theodore Weld put it, "the prophecy of Noah is the *vade mecum* of slaveholders, and they never venture abroad without it" (qtd. in H. Shelton Smith, *In His Image* 130).

An allegorical reading, by contrast, involves supplying context that is blatantly extrabiblical. In Northrop Frye's classic sense of the word, allegory involves "an 'abstract' approach which begins with the idea and then tries to find a concrete image to represent it" (89). Yet another example involves the Book of Genesis via the commentary of Adam Clarke. Here Dr. Cartwright enters the 1850s debate over the origins of black peoples:

> Fifty years ago, Dr. Adam Clark [sic], the learned commentator of the Bible, from deep reading in the Hebrew, Aramaic, and Coptic languages, was forced

to the conclusion that the creature which beguiled Eve was an animal formed like a man, walked erect, and had the gift of speech and reason. He believed it was an ourang-outang and not a serpent. If he had lived in Louisiana, instead of England, he would have recognized the *negro gardener*. (qtd. in Jenkins, 254).

As laughable as Cartwright's unmasking of the real identity of the serpent as a black gardener may be, he bases his remarks on Clarke's commentary, which is authoritative because of Clarke's supposed "deep reading in the Hebrew, Aramaic and Coptic languages." That such an unreasonable reading could come from an assumed basis in linguistic evidence gives us pause. Clarke's comment on a small snippet of Genesis 3:1 ("Now the serpent") is extensive indeed, running a full six pages (51–57), and it turns on his explication of the Hebrew word for serpent, *Nachash*. Yet Cartwright goes beyond even Clarke's fanciful linguistic gymnastics (which he confesses is based on an Arabic word and not actually on the Hebrew) when he insists that *Nachash* should be translated "negro." As Frye points out, "the basis of naive allegory is the mixed metaphor."

The other popular choice among slaveholders anxious to find concrete biblical imagery for the abstraction of black inferiority was the text of Genesis 9 referenced earlier, the so-called "curse of Ham." Interpretations designed to connect Ham linguistically with denotations of "blackness" and African physiological and geographical origins included the belief that Ham had copulated on the ark or that he committed miscegenation.[11]

GETTING THE WORD OUT: SLAVE MISSIONS, THE AMERICAN BIBLE SOCIETY, AND THE DEBATE OVER AFRICAN AMERICAN HERMENEUTICS

To what extent were nineteenth-century African Americans aware of the Bible Defense of Slavery? In order to assess African Americans' awareness of the debate over scripture and slavery, it is necessary to explore the availability of proslavery discourse and Bibles to free and enslaved African Americans before Emancipation. If enslaved people were not privy to the actual debates over slavery that ran in journals, periodicals, and books, they were certainly well acquainted with the proslavery racial hermeneutic. The dissemination of the proslavery biblical interpretation to enslaved men, women, and children was enacted by the slave missions movement, which began in South Carolina in the 1820s and 1830s.[12] While black attendance at missionary churches and gatherings was voluntary, white "missionaries"—most of whom were slaveholders themselves—were employed to reach out to the slave population with the gospel, embodying a contradiction of "evangelical belief and self-interested materialism" (Cornelius, *Slave Missions* 74).

These white "protectors"—reform-minded slave mission leaders—conform to what Riggins J. Earl calls "the ideal Christian master type" (15). The compromise and concessions to the slave system derived from a theology that separated the slave's body from his or her soul: "at best, this type of master could only say *theologically* that the slave's soul was created in the image of God. In no way could this belief change the master's *ethical* understanding of the nature of the slave as body" (15). In this way, the missions crafters preserved the image of the slave's body as having "utility value for the master's economic end" (915) while ameliorating their Christian consciences, pricked by the Great Commission of Jesus to "Go ye therefore, and teach all nations" (Matthew 28:11).

In an ironic twist, Nat Turner's revolutionary ideas, like those of Denmark Vesey and David Walker before him, regarded biblical texts as, in part, sources for black radicalism.[13] These Bible-sanctioned slave revolts stood in direct opposition to compromising reformers who insisted that "the Bible was a guarantor of peace, order, and stability on the plantation" (Cornelius 90). Vesey, Walker, and Turner internalized the strategy of biblical interpretation promoted by slavemasters and reinvested the Bible as a text of black agency and revolution, in a clash of private interpretations.

The attempt to dismantle the master's house using the master's tools, to paraphrase Audre Lorde, had serious consequences for African Americans, especially for their religious practices. Not only were black conspirators executed, but widespread and random white retaliatory violence ensued throughout black enslaved and free communities. Since both Vesey and, especially, Turner referred to the Bible in their justifications for their actions, African American Christianity became "black religion under white protection" (Cornelius, *Slave Missions*), as African Americans, slave and free, could not assemble even for religious purposes without the presence of a white overseer. This unfree worship gave rise to hush harbors and an underground black Christianity (see Raboteau, *Slave Religion*).

Most scholars assume a largely oral transmission of biblical texts among African Americans; in this respect, Carla Peterson's point in "*Doers of the Word*"—that orality and literacy be regarded as "not so much a dichotomy as a continuum, mutually interactive and illuminating" (60)—is well taken. It is in this sense that contemporary writer Toni Morrison refers to the Bible when she states that it "wasn't part of my reading, it was part of my life" (Taylor-Guthrie, *Conversations* 97). The desire to read permeates slave narratives, and the link between literacy and freedom has been well documented.[14] In *When I Can Read My Title Clear*, Janet D. Cornelius demonstrates the almost inextricable link between literacy and religion; the desire to read was, more often than not, a desire to read not just any book but the Protestant Bible.

A notable case of the desire for biblical literacy is none other than Frederick

Douglass, whose relationship to the Bible over his lifetime was at times ambivalent and contradictory. While much has been made of the revisions made to his three autobiographies, no one has commented on the changing representations of Douglass's view of the scriptures.[15] In his 1881 autobiography *Life and Times of Frederick Douglass*, he notes that his desire to read was specifically fueled by a desire to read the Bible: "The frequent hearing of my mistress reading the Bible aloud . . . awakened my curiosity in respect to this *mystery* of reading, and roused in me the desire to learn" (78). When Master Auld came in and put a stop to the reading lessons, Douglass quotes him in *Life and Times* as saying: "If he *learns to read the Bible* it will forever unfit him to be a slave" (79). This is in stark contrast to the famous literacy scene of his 1845 *Narrative*, where there is no specific mention of the Bible; instead, Douglass notes in this book simply that Mrs. Auld "commenced to teach me the A, B, C" (274). The Bible is also taken out of Mr. Auld's speech: "If you teach that nigger (speaking of myself) to read, there would be no keeping him. He would become unmanageable, and of no value to his master" (274).[16]

Why was any mention of the Bible as both the impetus for Douglass's desire for literacy and the slave master's fear excised from the 1845 text? I believe it is because the subject of African Americans and the Bible, highly contentious in 1845 when Douglass published his slave narrative, had ceased to be an issue in 1881, when he wrote *Life and Times*. Douglass's deliberate steering away from any mention of the Bible (and displaced mention of Nat Turner) in the earlier book, although possibly motivated by Garrison, reflects the embattled climate over this issue in the 1840s, as I will explore below.

While we might see this yearning for specifically biblical literacy as a desire for power—the need to appropriate the cultural authority and social cachet embodied by the Bible in nineteenth-century America—the sense of urgency in the desire for Bibles among slaves seems to have overreached such an explanation. As Cornelius summarizes: "Black Christians believed the Bible spoke to them in a special way, and they resented the slaveholders' abuse of God's word. Therefore, it was crucial that some people in the slave community gain reading skills, to 'take the Bible back,' to read what it really said" (86). Thus, in addition to seeing the Bible as a tool for liberation, slaves saw themselves as agents for liberating the Bible from oppressive, racially motivated hermeneutics. In order for the Bible to *be* the Bible, for most slaves, it needed first to be freed from its associations as the foundation and legitimation of the institution of slavery. By and large, African American hermeneutics in the nineteenth century was not motivated by a desire to de-authorize the Bible or question the Bible's claim to be the word of God, although such a demystifying discourse was available through both liberal northern abolitionists and southern ethnologists. Rather, they sought to de-authorize the master's unauthorized reading of the Bible as a racialized proslavery text. Thus, for African Americans, reading the Bible as *scripture* involved first unscripturing the master's discourse of black inferiority, which stood as the ground for proslavery ideology.

The "unscripturing" of the slavemaster's canon began as African Americans became armed with Bibles through the efforts of the American Bible Society (ABS), which was organized in 1816—the year in which, moreover, the African Methodist Episcopal Church was incorporated as the first black denomination in the United States.[17] The mission of the ABS was to distribute as widely as possible "the Holy Scriptures without note or comment" (qtd. in Gutjahr 30); thus, ABS Bibles contained neither notes nor pictures. Gutjhar describes the Bibles issued by ABS as

> small, about six by three and one-half inches, printed in a two-column style with chapters preceded by a short heading and a handful of short tables of information. The pages were almost completely devoid of margins, a sign of paper conservation. Finally, the Society bound these bibles in low-cost leather without elaborate spine or cover ornamentation. This small, sturdy bible edition was designed for function; a modest product inexpensively produced. (31)

In 1829, the Society printed 360,000 Bibles. By the 1860s they were printing over one million Bibles per year. Prices in the 1840s ranged from six cents for a New Testament to forty-five cents for an entire Bible (36). In contrast to the elaborately illustrated Bibles of the period sold to middle-class and wealthy whites, these relatively "blank" books left room for African Americans' imaginations to produce their own "illuminated" manuscripts, in accordance with their own interpretations of scripture.[18]

Colporteurs, the name given to ABS Bible distributors, who handed out Bibles personally, were particularly zealous to get Bibles into the hands of slaves and free blacks (Cornelius 113). Astonishingly, their efforts met with little resistance from slaveholders at first, many of whom actually requested Bibles, tracts, and even the formation of Sunday school groups for their slaves, even in states like Virginia, North Carolina, and Alabama, where it was against the law. If the claim that slavery rested on biblical authority were true, slaveholders should have nothing to fear in giving Bibles to slaves; indeed, it would appear suspect for them to withhold Bibles from enslaved people. As good "Christians," moreover, they would be held accountable for denying slaves religious instruction.

It is also within this mission to disseminate scriptures to slaves that a debate arose, which helps map the differing approach to scripture among African American leaders like Douglass, Bibb, and Garnet. The "Bibles for Slaves" campaign was not without contention. While one might imagine opposition within proslavery circles, there was also conflict over the policy in antislavery camps. First, the Bible was at the center of a major controversy between the

ABS and antislavery agencies, which produced a split in northern abolitionism and a division between important black abolitionists. The central irony in this debate is that it resulted from the ABS's opposition to growing sectarianism and its use of the Bible as a tool to promote unity and avoid secession. As Theodore Frelinghuysen, President of the ABS, stated in 1852, "If our country is safe, if the union is safe, if the people are safe, if the Church is safe, the Bible must have a hand in all of it" (qtd. in Cornelius 125).

The division among antislavery forces took place between those who feared that the campaign to provide slaves with Bibles (even with literacy) would constitute a half-measure that would dilute the abolitionist cause for black political freedom. Other abolitionists argued, conversely, for "literacy as the first step towards freedom and 'Bibles' as an attractive way to gain broader support for black liberation" (126). They reasoned that "slaveholders would be reluctant to keep literate, Bible-reading slaves in bondage" (130). Several agencies joined the ABS in this effort, including the American Tract Society (ATS) and the American Missionary Association (AMA). In 1848 the "Bibles for Slaves" campaign of the AMA enlisted the services of fugitive slave Henry Bibb in its cause. The goal was "to give a Bible or Testament to every slave who could read" (131). However, Bibb and the campaign of the American Missionary Association were soon attacked by other black abolitionists, primarily by the preeminent Frederick Douglass.

Douglass's opposition to the American Missionary Association and Henry Bibb had two sources. First, Bible Society reports that slaves were being taught to read blunted Douglass's insistence on the cruelty and deprivation of the system of chattel slavery. Although he himself had been taught to read while a slave, Douglass flat-out denied the Tract Society's report of slaves being taught by colporteurs, who had become "permanent missionaries" on some plantations. Douglass viewed the Bibles for Slaves campaign as "a sham, a delusion, and a snare" (qtd. in Cornelius 131). On closer inspection, Douglass did not object to the Bible per se, even conceived of as the Word of God, but of its connection to slavery: "The Bible is peculiarly the companion of liberty," he wrote. "It belongs to a new order of things—slavery is of the old—and will only be made worse by an attempt to mend it with the Bible" (qtd. in Cornelius 131). Arguing in the vein of rationalist, northern liberalism, Douglass went on to say that to give slaves Bibles constituted a perverse form of cruelty:

> Away with all trifling with the man in fetters! Give a hungry man a stone, and tell what beautiful houses are made of it,—give ice to a freezing man and tell him of its good properties in hot weather,—throw a drowning man a dollar, as a mark of your good will,—but do not mock the bondman in his misery, by giving him a Bible when he cannot read it. (qtd. in Cornelius 132)

Obviously Douglass's comments are predicated on the need for literacy, without which, as he suggests, the Bible is about as useful as a "stone." Here Douglass deliberately echoes the words of Jesus in Luke 11:11: "if a son shall ask bread of any of you that is a father, will he give him a stone?" Douglass uses the same rhetorical strategy as Jesus in this parable of an absurd example, designed to provoke a powerful response in the hearer. Douglass was also, as Callahan points out, concerned that, given the climate of the Bible defense of slavery, Bibles would be used for proslavery propaganda: "The master, holding the Bible and the whip, would now wield each in the service of the other" (24). One can read the appendix to Douglass's 1845 *Narrative*, in which he skillfully distinguishes between "Christianity proper" and the "slaveholding Christianity of this land," as a proactive strike against just such religious indoctrination.

Henry Bibb agreed with the philosophy of the Bibles for Slaves proponents, believing that the Bible could be understood by even semi- or functionally literate slaves and ex-slaves. As Cornelius points out, slaves were "bringing meaning to the text," combining "the knowledge they carried inside them with the letters on the printed page" (94). Many accounts of literacy include the commonly held belief that God himself would teach slaves to read; if they could just get their hands on a Bible, God would provide the literacy, supernaturally if necessary. Shaker eldress Rebecca Cox Jackson, for example, argues that God directly taught her to read in her autobiography, *Gifts of Power*.[19]

Thomas Lewis Johnson recounts his experience with literacy in 1836 in his slave narrative *Twenty-Eight Years a Slave*:

> There was a box of old books stored away in a lumber room, and amongst these books was a large Bible. I took this Bible to my room, and day after day, when I had finished my work in the house, and had a little time to spare, I would go to my room, lock myself in, and try to read the Bible, commencing at Genesis and calling over the letters of each word I could not understand as follows:—"In the b-e-g-i-n-n-i-n-g God c-r-e-a-t-e-d the heaven and the earth"; and thus I struggled on from day to day.

This account of painstaking acquisition of literacy did not deter slaves from reading and interpreting the Bible for themselves in an act of defiance against the proslavery hermeneutic.

Debates over the Bibles for Slaves initiative came to a head in 1849 in New York City. In fact, two debates were staged. The first included Henry Highland Garnet and Samuel Ringhold Ward, who supported the cause against Charles L. Reason, a black oppositionist. The next evening, however, featured Garnet and Bibb versus Douglass himself. Bibb and Garnet proved no match for Douglass's fierce oratorical and persuasive gifts. The debate resulted in a shouting match that threatened to split the abolitionist cause. Bibb finally abandoned his work with Bibles for Slaves and emigrated to Canada.

Money continued to be contributed to the AMA's Bibles for Slaves drive from 1849–54, mostly from the midwestern and New England states. The argument in favor of the campaign followed the lines of a split between the enslaved body and the (potentially) free spirit, assuming that political liberation could take decades while the need for Bibles to promote salvation and spiritual liberation was immediate. Although the campaign offered no immediate political relief for African Americans, most slaves valued the presentation of Bibles as worthy in and of itself. Thus, slaves often shared the same understanding of scriptures as the ABS. In a popular pamphlet widely distributed by the ABS, a slave named William reported:

> God teach me to read.... God give me desire to read, and that make reading easy. Master give me a Bible, and one sailor show me the letters, and so me learn to read by myself, with God's goot help.... Me read all about Jesus Christ, and how he loved sinners, and wicked men kill him, and he died, and came again from the grave, and all this for poor Negro. (qtd. in Cornelius 112)

This "centripedal reading" experience, to borrow Wesley Kort's phrase, which personalized the literal narrative of Christ's birth, death, burial, and resurrection, was of intrinsic worth to African Americans seeking, in a way that defined their humanity, spiritual redemption in the Christian gospel.

THE LITERAL/LITERARY SENSE: TOWARD AN AFRICAN AMERICAN PUBLIC HERMENEUTICS

In the story of Balaam, chapters 22–24 of Numbers actually records his prophecy and stages an interplay between competing discourses of power and authority. Just as the incident with the talking donkey reversed the power relations between master and beast of burden, the account of his actual prophecy is a battle between authorized and de-authorized uses of language. In the tale of Balaam and the ass, the Angel of the Lord represents divinity itself, intervening in Balaam's path. More important, the Angel stands for power to use and interpret sacred language; the God who "opened the donkey's mouth to speak" is the same God to whom Balaam owes his prophetic gift and allegiance, notwithstanding his role as a prophet-for-hire with Balak. While Balak has paid for a curse—the appropriation of divine language for the purpose of conquest—the presence of the Angel of the Lord is a reminder to Balaam of who it is that gives him the power to speak at all.

A repetitious series of incidents ensues along classic folktale motifs, as Robert Alter points out, demonstrating that "the Bible's polemic monotheism can produce high comedy" (*Art of Biblical Narrative* 105). After thrice having Balak build seven altars and sacrifice seven bulls, presumably to give Balaam greater communication with the divine, Balaam announces, "I have no power to say whatever I want. I will speak only the message that God puts in my mouth" (Numbers 22:38, NLT). Trying to get his money's worth, Balak brings Balaam to different mountains, assuming that a better view will change the direction of his speech; but Balaam stubbornly refuses to curse Israel, saying, "I will tell you whatever he [God] reveals to me" (23:3). Thus, prophetic utterance is not about fortune-telling, nor is it subject to the demands of the market; instead, it resides in its agreement with Divine utterance. To Balak's angry retort, "I brought you to curse my enemies. Instead you have blessed them," Balaam responds rhetorically, "How can I curse those whom God has blessed?"(23:11, 8). To turn cursing into blessing is really to *return* to the original pronouncement of the *imago dei*.[20]

In contrast to private interpretation, then, I propose a category of public hermeneutics closely akin to what Hans W. Frei terms the *sensus literalis*, "the closest one can come to a consensus reading of the Bible as the sacred text in the Christian Church" ("Literal Reading" 37). Inquiring about the future of the literal reading in light of Ricoeur's phenomenology and deconstruction, Frei asks of a current, revised form of *sensus literalis*, "does it stretch or will it break?" While there are criticisms that the category of the literal reading remains somewhat elusive and undefined in Frei, the category is predicated on the notion that it was due to the "centrality of the story of Jesus that the Christian interpretive tradition in the West gradually assigned clear primacy to the literal sense in the reading of scripture."[21] It is thus commitment to the literal, base-line narrative of Jesus that legitimates other "legitimate" reading strategies, including tropological, allegorical, analogical, and other approaches. According to Frei, these types of readings, especially when applied to what Christians call the Old Testament or Hebrew Bible, "could only be done because the story of Jesus itself was taken to have a literal or plain meaning. He was the Messiah, and the fourfold storied depiction in the gospels, especially of his passion and resurrection, was the enacted form of his identity as Messiah" (37). Moreover, the literal understanding of Jesus's narrative was not descriptive, but rather ascriptive: "That 'Jesus'—not someone else or nobody in particular—is the subject, the agent and patient of these stories is said to be their crucial point, and the descriptives of events, sayings, personal qualities, and so forth, become literal by being firmly predicated of him" (42).

An example of what I mean by private and public reading is discussed by Mark A. Noll in "The Image of the United States as a Biblical Nation, 1776–1865." Noll contrasts the use of scripture by ministers to promote the idea of the United

States as a "biblical nation" with the dissenting view of "enslaved Christians" whose approach to Scripture was "not bound by American nationalism." On the one hand, "Ministers prepared and delivered sermons on a text of Scripture, but this text of Scripture became a gateway not for the proclamation of essentially biblical messages, but for the minister's social, political, or cultural convictions, which had been securely in place long before he had turned to the Bible" (42). For Christian slaves, on the other hand, "it was the Bible-as-story which captured the imagination" (49). Noll's insistence on the narrative quality of the Bible accords with Frei's promotion of the literal sense as essentially about its narrativity, grounded in the life, death, burial, and resurrection of Jesus Christ. It is in this hermeneutical spirit that we find African American women refuting proslavery claims in largely representational form—narrative, fiction, and poetry—as the case of Frances E. W. Harper demonstrates.

WORDS MADE FLESH: THE BIBLE DEFENSE OF SLAVERY AND THE POETRY OF FRANCES E. W. HARPER

In 1901, at the age of seventy-five, noted African American writer, speaker, and abolitionist Frances Ellen Watkins Harper published a slim volume of verse called *Idylls of the Bible*. It was self-published, judging from the address on the title page: "Philadelphia: 1006 Bainbridge Street," Harper's private residence since 1871. The small volume begins with a revision of an early poem, *Moses: A Story of the Nile*. Following a brief essay and two sentimental poems, however, the majority of the text is consumed with the passion, death, and resurrection of Jesus Christ: "Christ's Entry into Jerusalem," "The Resurrection of Jesus," "Simon's Countrymen," "Simon's Feast."[22] That the base-line narrative of the life, death, and resurrection of Jesus—including his encounters with Mary and Simon, a woman and an African, during the course of events leading to his crucifixion—should loom so large in her poetic vision late in her life attests to the centrality of biblical narrative in any assessment of her writing, in particular her poetry. Since Frances Smith Foster's restoration of Harper to the African American and women's literary canon in 1990 with the publication of the anthology *A Brighter Coming Day*, the majority of criticism on Harper has been concerned with her only novel, *Iola Leroy*. Harper's poetry has been treated most extensively by Foster, Melba Joyce Boyd, Maryemma Graham, and Carla Peterson, though only Boyd devotes an entire book to her poetic vision. Of her poetry, the long epic *Moses: A Story of the Nile* has received the most commentary.[23] While the relative neglect of Harper's biblical poetry can be attributed to what Frances Smith Foster calls the triad of "gender, genre and vulgar secularism," here I would like to focus on two poems that feature her poetic response to the Bible defense of slavery.

Harper was born free in Baltimore in 1825. She was orphaned at three years of age and raised by her maternal uncle, William Watkins, who ran an academy for Negro youth. The rigorous curriculum for the academy included "daily study of the bible . . . History, Geography, Mathematics, English, Natural Philosophy, Greek, Latin, Music, and Rhetoric" (Boyd 36). William Watkins was very active in antislavery causes, and his son, William J. Watkins, assisted Frederick Douglass with his abolitionist paper, *The North Star* (Boyd 37). In 1850–52, Harper held teaching positions at Union Seminary in Wilberforce, Ohio, and Little York, Pennsylvania. In 1854, *Poems* was published in Boston, and Harper began a long career as a speaker as she joined the antislavery lecture circuit. She married Fenton Harper in 1860, and their one daughter, Mary, was born in 1862 (Fenton Harper had three other children from a previous marriage). They settled on a farm in Columbus, Ohio, until she was widowed in 1864 and returned to Baltimore the following year. Two Reconstruction lecture tours—1867–69 and 1869–71—took Harper to Georgia, Florida, Alabama, Mississippi, Louisiana, North Carolina, Virginia, Kentucky, Tennessee, Missouri, Delaware, and Maryland. Harper drew heavily on her experiences during these travels in her only novel, *Iola Leroy, or Shadows Uplifted*, published in 1892. In 1871 Harper settled in Pennsylvania with her daughter, Mary, who preceded her in death in 1909. Harper died in Pennsylvania in 1911.

The public debate format staged between proslavery and antislavery forces, in both oral and published form, was probably the vehicle through which Frances E. W. Harper learned of "The Bible Defence of Slavery."[24] It is this poem and another, "The Dismissal of Tyng," which reports a church's disfellowshipping of a congregant who makes proslavery statements during a worship service, that demonstrate Harper's acute awareness of the use of the Bible for proslavery arguments.[25] Taken together, these poems situate Harper's biblicopoetics within the debate over proslavery biblical justifications and the vexed issue of the relationship between slavery and Christianity in general. The poems are linked verbally by the repetition of a key phrase:

> Remember Slavery's cruel hands
> Make heathens at your door!
> *("Bible Defence of Slavery," lines 23–24)*

and

> 'Tis right to plead for heathen lands,
>   To send the Bible to their shores,
> And then to make, for power and pelf,
>   A race of heathen at our door
> *("The Dismissal of Tyng," lines 13–16)*

The celebration of Tyng's dismissal from a local church may have been based on an actual incident. In any event, it represents Harper's affirmative answer to the classic debate question rendered as a subtitle to the 1846 volume *A Debate on Slavery*: "Is slave-holding in itself sinful, and the relation between master and slave, a sinful relation?"[26] The debate, which occurred in Cincinnati in 1845 between Rev. Blanchard and Dr. Rice, included a discussion on the denial of Christian fellowship to slaveholders, a topic hotly debated in a number of Christian denominations and local churches. Rice, representing the proslavery side of the debate, states:

> I maintain, that the Methodist church never has excluded men from the church, simply because they were slave-holders. Although that church has been divided by the question of slavery, even the northern division of it has not yet made slave-holding a bar to Christian fellowship. And the same may be said of every denomination of Christians of respectable size in our country. Some small churches have excluded slave-holders from their communion; but their numbers in the slave States are extremely small. And this fact shows the tendency of abolitionism even in its mildest form to take the gospel from both masters and slaves. (400–401)

In Harper's poem, the equation of the Christian/heathen opposition with white/black is a function of the system of slavery; by withholding Bibles and Christianity from enslaved peoples, Harper suggests, one renders them permanently "heathens" and outsiders.

In Harper's poetic canon, twenty-two works are based on direct exegesis of a sustained passage from the Bible. Another ten have biblical titles but are not direct interpretations of a text. Of the twenty-two biblical poems, fourteen are from New Testament passages; all of these feature Jesus and are based specifically on the Gospel narratives. This problematizes the general view that African Americans are an "Old Testament people," with the Exodus motif as the central and dominant point of biblical engagement.[27] Moreover, Harper's New Testament emphasis is centered on the Gospels and the person of Jesus. This is an implicit corrective to the proslavery canon, which emphasizes select portions of Genesis and the Pauline epistles.[28] The only proslavery argument involving Jesus declared that Jesus did not explicitly talk about slavery and thus must not have been against it.[29] It is also significant that the most serious biblical stumbling block for slaveholding biblicists from the late eighteenth century and after proved to be Jesus's teaching of the Golden Rule, a passage quoted in every antislavery biblical argument. Therefore, Harper's invocation of Jesus is neither arbitrary nor gratuitous, but rather a purposeful refutation of the logic of proslavery biblical discourse.

Yet, while Harper's choice of biblical subject revoices the abolitionist biblical argument, she evidences a more comprehensive Christology and biblical vision than did antislavery debaters, who tended to rely on stock arguments and texts. Thus, Harper's biblical poems are not simply versified antislavery speeches, but rather they exhibit an intimacy in the portrayal of Jesus that exceeds the desire to appropriate the Bible for political ends. On the other hand, Harper does not simply retell the Bible stories; instead, she makes choices of detail and structure that are designed to lift the text off the page and into the imagination, hearts, and minds of readers. While "Bible Defence of Slavery" and "The Dismissal of Tyng" show Harper's familiarity with proslavery hermeneutics, her undoing of racial hermeneutics is accomplished through her other poems on Bible stories, particularly those depicting biblical women interacting with the figure of Christ. By focusing on her religious poems, usually regarded as important yet subordinate to her more political expressions, one cannot help but notice the intimacy of her depictions of Jesus, especially in the poetry involving women subjects. Jesus is bodily present in her poetry. One critic describes Harper's Jesus as "a soothing source of peace and transcendence" (Boyd 71), yet the Jesus of Harper's religious poems is incredibly immanent, as evidenced by the predominance of language of touch in the poems. One example of this is the opening poem in the 1854 *Poems on Miscellaneous Subjects*, "The Syrophenecian Woman," which recounts the Canaanite woman's persistent petition for her daughter's deliverance.[30] Another example is "Saved by Faith," which retells the pericope of the Woman with the Issue of Blood from the synoptic gospels.

The women in both of these stories transgress boundaries of gender that would limit women's conversation with men in public, let alone physical contact. Moreover, both pericopes are embedded in first-century animosities between Jews and Gentiles, the main "racial" division and marker of difference in the Gospels. Jesus thus refers to the woman with the issue of blood as "Daughter," indicating her Jewishness, and to the Gentile woman simply as "woman." The Syrophenician woman, as a Gentile, is doubly "other" by virtue of both race and gender. In the other story, however, the woman is referred to as "diseased" (Matthew 9:20); in a religious context, she would be doubly unclean and thus also untouchable. Both women, then, represent extreme outsidedness and social alienation.

Harper makes excellent dramatic use of these circumstances as she emphasizes, in both poems, Jesus's nearness and availability to the most socially othered. In "The Syrophenician Woman," for example, she writes twice in the first two stanzas (presumably from the woman's first person perspective) that "Judea's prophet draweth near!" (line 2) and "Now the prophet draweth near" (line 7). Having set up the expectation of deliverance, however, the anguished appeal of the woman is met with silence: "Jesus answered not a word" (line 12). It is at this point that the woman assumes a posture that would have been recognizable to virtually every nineteenth-century reader of this poem:

> With a purpose naught could move,
> And the seal of woman's love,
> Down she knelt in anguish wild—
> "Master! save, Oh! save my child!" (lines 13–16)

Jean Fagan Yellin has written at length about the prominence of the antislavery emblem "Am I Not a Man and a Brother" and its female counterpart "Am I Not a Woman and a Sister," which depict a kneeling bondman or bondwoman with hands outstretched in a petition for freedom.[31] Here, in the centermost stanza of a seven-stanza poem, Harper references the iconography of the female antislavery emblem. In the original texts, we are told that the woman "worshipped him" (Matthew 15:25) and "fell at his feet" (Mark 7:25), but Harper's careful description, even using the terminology "the seal of woman's love," would have been blatant to any contemporary reader.

Yet Harper's application of the story to contemporary abolitionism stops short of de-authorizing the biblical account; rather than read "against the grain" of the original pericope, she simply exposes to view the subversiveness inherent in its textuality. Jesus explains to the woman that his primary mission is to "Israel's lost and scattered sheep," which seems to reify the racial/cultural hierarchy of Jew over Gentile. Harper is not inverting the biblical story here; the very inversion and transgression she is trying to promote are already present in the biblical narrative. The Syrophenician woman's subversion of the social discourse of hierarchy takes place in her witty punning off of Jesus's metaphorical reference to "the children's bread" (line 18; see also Matthew 15:26 and Mark 7:27). Jesus's use of the word "dog" is both metaphorical and literal, as he mimics (for didactic purposes to his disciples) the discourse of othering that referred to women and gentiles as "dogs." The woman's witty retort, revoicing even her own outside position by laying claim, ironically, to the word "dogs," renames her petition for help as a seeking after "crumbs."

Yet it is Harper's portrayal of Jesus as the source of miraculous deliverance and power that invests this poem with biblical authority; the woman seeks Jesus because "sickness and sorrow before him depart" (line 4). Even after the overlaying of the antislavery icon, the woman continues to appeal to Christ, because "True and faithful is thy word" (line 22). Having proclaimed the authority of Jesus's word, the woman's "but" in line 23 simply opens a space for inclusivity: "But the humblest, meanest, may / Eat the crumbs they cast away" (lines 23–24). Jesus's response, however, exceeds her expectations. Not only does he promise the granting of her petition, but exclaims "be it even as thy word!" (line 26), investing her words with power. The power of the Gentile woman's words, "Thou hast ask'd, and shall prevail" (line 28), derives from her acknowledgment that Jesus's words are "true and faithful."

Harper's biblical poems enter the debate over slavery on precisely the terrain of "cultural hermeneutics" (Noll, *America's God* 395). Like Harper, other African American women writers made use of the Bible in spite of its (mis)use in defending slavery. The chapters in part two will explore a range of black women transforming scriptures in prayers and meditations, novels, and poetry.

PART TWO

transforming scriptures

※※※※※※※※※※※※※※※※※※※※※※※※※※※※※※

*But we all, with open face beholding as in a glass the glory
of the Lord, are changed into the same image from glory to glory,
even as by the Spirit of the Lord.*
  2 Corinthians 3:18

What did nineteenth-century African American women writers *do* with the Bible?

African American women writers were profoundly aware of the hermeneutical and theological difficulties created by the Bible defense of slavery in the nineteenth century. Rather than engage in the type of point-by-point debate held by Frederick Douglass, Henry Bibb, and other black male abolitionists, black women in the nineteenth century chose to dismantle the Bible defense through literary representation in genres like poetry, fiction, and even spiritual narrative and written prayers.

The chapters in this section begin with the prayers/meditations of Maria W. Stewart, as she demonstrates the sweeping range of black women's biblicism as cultural performance. Branching out from the Balaam and Shulamite tropes, Hannah Crafts and Harriet E. Wilson make use of the figures of Esther, the Queen of Sheba, and Joseph, expanding the terms by which African Americans appropriate biblical self-representations. Harriet E. Wilson challenges the gender boundaries of black feminist hermeneutics by signifying on the Joseph narrative of Genesis. Finally, Sherley Anne Williams and Toni Morrison reprise the Shulamite trope as they engage the Bible for their formulations of black female sexuality in the contemporary period.

CHAPTER THREE

sampling the scriptures

MARIA W. STEWART AND THE GENRE OF PRAYER

As the subtitle of historian Marilyn Richardson's 1987 edition of Maria W. Stewart's essays and speeches suggests, Stewart entered the historical and literary canon as "America's First Black Woman Political Writer." Accordingly, Richardson includes only one of Stewart's religious meditations in the appendix to that edition. More recent treatments of Stewart have retrieved Stewart's religious writings and reconnected them to her canon. *Spiritual Narratives*—the 1988 volume of the Schomburg Library, edited by Susan Houchins—includes the full text of Stewart's 1835 *Productions* with the religious material intact. Consequently, more recent studies, like Carla Peterson's *"Doers of the Word"* and Joycelyn Moody's *Sentimental Confessions*, include readings of the religious *Meditations*, which accounts for a significant portion of Stewart's writings. Cedric May's recent book reads Stewart's writings in the context of evangelism and black resistance.[1]

Following Peterson and Moody, I regard Stewart primarily as a religious writer. Moreover, by placing her *Meditations* at the center of her discourse, rather than at the margins, I locate her unique style in the context of African American oral and performative culture. As cultural performance, Stewart uses the Bible both as "a source of self-empowerment, an authorization to act in the world" (Peterson 56), and as a part of the "black jeremiad" that views spirituality through the lens of social justice (Moody 29). Stewart, indeed, "fashioned for herself a public identity as a prophet" (May 117), and her use of the Bible as a primary source for her writings is part of her prophetic persona and cultural performance. This type of writing/reading, which I will call "literary sampling," is deeply embedded in African American culture, particularly musical performance. By extension, the intertextual dimension of "sampling" informs African American religious culture—sermons, spirituals, hymns, and so forth—and the genre of performative prayer. By "performative prayer" I mean especially those prayers "composed" for public performance in African American worship and/

or written for publication, and that are thus connected to a different ethos of community, ownership, and language than privatized utterance. Language as communal property informs call and response, spirituals, blues, and African American oral culture. In *Race Music*, Guthrie Ramsey describes the rhetorical power of black gospel music as a fundamental hybridity based on "stylistic juxtapositionings" (191). Thus, literary sampling resembles signifying, pastiche, and other types of intertextual tropes. Yet in addition to the deliberate playing against the grain of the original that is signifying, literary sampling utilizes the original text as a vehicle for the expression of private and communal emotions. In other words, literary sampling may look backward to the original and/or forward, emphasizing instead the new creative product.

In "Interpreting Biblical Scholarship for the Black Church Traditions," Thomas Hoyt Jr. defines "proof-texting" as "taking a text completely out of context in order to validate one's own subjective views (pretexts) or one's understanding of doctrine, tradition and the like" (19–21). This is close to what I referred to as "private interpretation" in chapter two; however, private interpretation is more strategic in its aim to oppress and exclude. Unlike proof-texting, where ignorance of context is elided, sampling scripture showcases the virtuosity of the sampler as s/he composes a "new song." Stewart's use of biblical material does not simply use biblical texts to "prove" a prior assumption, but rather constitutes the creative use of a presumably creative Word.

Born free in 1803 in Hartford, Connecticut, Maria Miller married James Stewart on August 10, 1826, in a ceremony performed in Boston's First African American Baptist Church by the pastor R. Thomas Paul. James Stewart died on December 17, 1829, forcing Maria to sue for his long overdue pension from service in the War of 1812. She lost the case. Influenced by, among others, the fiery black abolitionist and early black nationalist David Walker, who died a suspicious death in 1830 after the publication of the third edition of his inflammatory *Appeal*, Stewart launched out on a public speaking career in Boston that lasted three years. This move into the previously forbidden space of the lecture platform (Stewart was the first American-born woman to deliver a public address to a mixed-gender audience) was precipitated by a new experience of religious conversion, which began a series of "spiritual interrogations" between Stewart and God Himself.

During her Boston years, Stewart published two pamphlets that were later collected into one volume: in 1831, *Religion and the Pure Principles of Morality, the Sure Foundation on Which We Must Build*, her most sustained political and theological analysis; and in 1832, *Meditations*, a series of shorter writings. In 1832–33, she delivered four public lectures that were printed in William Lloyd Garrison's abolitionist paper *The Liberator*. These writings and speeches, far from making Stewart a community hero, ostracized her from the very community she felt called to serve, and she moved to New York in 1834. It was there that her *Productions of Mrs. Maria Stewart* was assembled, including both pamphlets and the four previously printed speeches, and published in one volume in 1835.[2]

Stewart's positioning of the 1832 text of *Meditations* centermost in *Productions* is significant. Moreover, with seven of the twenty-one short writings of *Meditations* composed in the genre of written public prayer, I would suggest that any new assessment of her writings should begin by considering prayer central, and not peripheral, to her work and to her overall analysis of the class, race, and gender dynamics of African American culture and history. Stewart's forays into the religious genres of prayer and meditation, and the authority and mastery she exhibits with scripture, are evidence of her significant investment in cultural and intellectual work. The choice of contemplative genres like prayer and mediation (and even the essay)[3] seems out of sync with African American women's labor north of slavery, which was usually domestic work leaving little time or place for intellectual and spiritual work.[4] "Meditation" is a word that signifies both spiritually and intellectually, and it reminds us that Stewart's writings, while religious, are not "other-worldly" but rather are intellectual works. In the introduction to *Meditations* (1832), Stewart writes: "I have borrowed much of my language from the Holy Bible. During the years of childhood and youth, it was the book that I most studied; and now, while my hands are toiling for their daily sustenance, my heart is most generally meditating upon its divine truths" (24). Notice here the use of the words "studied" and "meditating"—even in the midst of physical labor—as Stewart expresses her awareness of the intellectual activity of her "heart."[5] Indeed the juxtaposition of "hands" and "heart"—of "toiling for . . . daily sustenance" and "meditating upon . . . divine truths"—challenges Western notions of intellectual labor as a product of the economy of leisure. This transgression of the class parameters of literary production is instructive, as it must challenge our own frameworks and the intellectual categories that we would bring to Stewart's work.

THE GENRE OF PRAYER

> One factor in the creation of atmospheres I have included—the preliminary prayer. The prayer leader was sometimes a woman. It was the prayer leader who directly prepared the way for the sermon, set the scene, as it were. . . . These preliminary prayers were often products hardly less remarkable than the sermons.
> James Weldon Johnson, *God's Trombones*

In his 1927 collection of sermonic poems, *God's Trombones*, James Weldon Johnson documents the African American religious practice of the "preliminary prayer," which precedes the sermon in African American worship. Almost incidentally, he remarks that "the prayer leader was sometimes a woman," a choice role amid the general atmosphere of gender exclusion marked out for black women's voices.[6] The high value accorded to the prayer leader and her/his prayer stems from the aesthetic and spiritual value of prayer. According to Johnson's eyewitness testimony, prayer leaders produced oral "texts hardly less remarkable" than the much-anticipated sermon, around which the entire worship service was usually constructed.[7] It is interesting, however, that in documenting the cultural use of public prayer and the value accorded such compositions, Johnson assigns prayer to "atmosphere" and "set[ting] the scene," rather than understanding it as a cultural force in its own right. And so we turn to Maria Stewart's seven written public prayers in *Meditations* confronted with the dilemma of prayer as a recognized formal and cultural product that has been undertheorized.

Stewart's penchant for the written prayer, embedding many prayers within her essays and speeches, could very well mean that she had served the congregation at First African Baptist in just such a capacity as female prayer leader. The virtuosity of her prayers, which, as I will show below, are unique and among the finest of contemporary examples, bespeaks a writer/pray-er experienced in the art of public praying. Many of the prayers refer to her pastor and church, and, while she may have gained a reputation for being a fine prayer leader, they have the effect of one praying for her enemies and "for those who despitefully use you" (Matthew 5:44). In fact, the writing down of her prayers could easily be a sign that a public pulpit was no longer open to her, and so the written text became the outlet for a mode of expression that was natural and important to her but had to be displaced onto the printed page.

There is, however, a long tradition of written prayers by African Americans reclaimed by James Melvin Washington in his edited volume *Conversations with God*. Washington collected 190 prayers spanning 235 years; some were individually published as broadsides and pamphlets, while others came from sermons, slave narratives and testimonies, spiritual narratives, diaries and journals, the abolitionist press, and novels. "A satisfactory comparative history and anthropology of prayer had yet to be written," writes Washington. "African American prayers as a literary genre and a religious social practice, assume that God is just and loving and that the human dilemma is that we cannot always experience and see God's justice and love" (xlvi). In analyzing prayer as a literary genre, I will focus on the use of biblical allusions and quotations in prayer by composers from 1760 to 1860.

Marilyn Richardson contends that Stewart's use of biblical passages and hymns in her texts was "commonplace to the audience she addressed" (xvii) and "common with preachers and religious writers of her day" (15). While they are more sympathetic to her religious views, Peterson and Moody also treat

Stewart's Bible references as marginal and peripheral. Even a cursory examination of the prayers of Stewart's forerunners and contemporaries, however, reveals striking differences in Stewart's style, especially with regard to the use of scripture and biblical allusion. While other pray-ers regularly quote the Bible, sometimes at length, Stewart's use of biblical material goes beyond mere quotation to the echo and reverberation, the creative re-use of selective phrases of scripture—probably, as Peterson has observed, from memory (60)—arranged for an overall effect.[8] A brief exploration of other recorded prayers written just before or during Stewart's time will suffice to illustrate this point.

The first written prayer collected by Washington is the long metrical poem *An Evening Thought, Salvation by Christ, with Penitential Cries*, published by enslaved poet Jupiter Hammon in 1760.[9] While Hammon's verse-prayer is biblically informed, it is not dependent on actual phrases, rhythms, and intonations from the Bible itself. In fact, *An Evening Thought* more closely resembles a hymn, especially since the headnote, which forms a part of the original title, states that it was "Composed by Jupiter Hammon." Somewhat ironically, it is Hammon's second poem, rather than the prayer-poem, that takes a step toward the scriptural sampling that will come to mark Stewart's use of the prayer genre.

An Address to Miss Phillis Wheatley, Ethiopian Poetess, in Boston is dated "Hartford, August 4, 1778," and it begins its versified tribute to the first African American woman poet with an epistolary address, "Miss Wheatley; pray give leave to express as follows."[10] Hammon's polite gendering of Wheatley, conferring on her the social markers of womanhood, should be appreciated in light of the denial of womanhood to African American women by the larger society. Thus, in an intracommunal frame of reference, Hammon's recognition of Wheatley's womanhood can be read as a transgressive act. What follows is a twenty-one-stanza poem (each stanza conveniently numbered), again arranged in fourteeners, with alternating rhyme (abab, cdcd, etc.). What is interesting for my purposes is the printed marginalia of the poem, assigning a biblical reference for twenty of the twenty-one stanzas, with the word "Death" assigned to stanza number five, one of several stanzas in which Hammon alludes to the Middle Passage.[11] Hammon's portrayal of each segment of Wheatley's biography—which, in broad outline, forms a part of the full title of the Address—inscribes Wheatley's life history into the biblical text. At the poem's end are appended the following remarks: "Composed by Jupiter Hammon, a Negro Man belonging to Mr. Joseph Lloyd, of Queen's Village on Long Island, now in Hartford. The above lines are published by the Author, a number of his friends, who desire to join with him in their regards to Miss Wheatley."

While some of the biblical references in the margins of the *Address* relate thematically or via paraphrase to the corresponding verse stanza, many appear to have no discernible relationship. Several of the passages cited from Psalms, for example, appear to be general praises to God for his goodness and protection, and they are usually appended to stanzas of the poem that mention salvation or the "merciful enslavement" ideology of the era, almost as if Hammon is trying to construct Wheatley's (or other readers') reaction to the content of the stanza—as if orchestrating praise in call/response fashion. Moreover, the allusions are clumped together and evidence nothing of the range of scriptural knowledge and use of Stewart's writings. At best, the scriptural allusions refer to a paraphrased biblical passage, tailored to fit the context, rhyme scheme, and meter of the poem, rather than making use of actual biblical phraseology.

Hammon's near contemporaries, Congregationalist preacher Lemuel Haynes and Wheatley, also wrote prose prayers that rely on paraphrase rather than direct quotation. Haynes's "A Prayer for New Birth," published in 1776, the year of the "birth" of the new nation of the United States of America, seems deliberately to bypass the language of the Revolution as he ends his prayer by referencing a different kingdom, one founded on the individual's relationship with God rather than on a national identity based on the liberal ideology of the individual: "having the kingdom of Christ set up in our hearts here, may we grow up to the stature of perfect men in Christ Jesus" (6; see Ephesians 4:13). Wheatley, in "A Mother's Prayer for the Child in Her Womb" (1779), pleads for God's mercy on the unborn infant "[t]hough conceived in Sin and [brought] forth in iniquity" (7), which references Psalm 51, one of the penitential psalms.[12] Interestingly, it represents a reorientation of the idea of birth from a spiritual to a natural frame of reference.

Prayers written by African American preachers Richard Allen and Absalom Jones, who were responsible for the formation of the African Methodist Episcopal Church, the first African American Christian denomination in the United States, more closely approximate Stewart's. This is significant because they were writing during a time when African American community and culture were being formed, following the abolition of the transatlantic slave trade of 1808. In "A Prayer for Hope," for example, Allen quotes the Old Testament Wisdom poem Job ("Yet I undoubtedly know my Redeemer lives, and shall raise me up at the last day" [10]), and the minor prophet Habakkuk ("Although the fig-tree shall not blossom, neither shall fruit be in the vines; although the labor of the olive shall fail, and the fields yield no meat; although the flock shall be cut off from the fold, and there shall be no herd in the stalls, yet I will rejoice in the Lord, I will joy in the God of my salvation" [10]). Absalom Jones's "Thanksgiving Prayer for the Abolition of the African Slave Trade," which forms part of his sermon of 1808, includes direct quotation or allusion to ten biblical verses.[13] Significantly, six of Jones's allusions are two passages from the Old Testament prophets, four from Isaiah alone, and one from the New Testament Apocalypse, or Revelation.

A similar use of the Bible appears in the prayers of Daniel Alexander Payne, who became bishop of the AME Church in 1841. His "Prayer for Dedication of a Church Edifice" (1848) includes multiple scriptural references, but all are highly contextual. Beginning by invoking Solomon's prayer for the dedication of the temple in Jerusalem in 1 Kings 8 ("And now, O, Lord God, Most High, whom the heaven, and heaven of heavens cannot contain"), the prayer proceeds through allusions to other topical verses concerning church/temple buildings, church ordinances, sacraments, and missions. There is little here to connect the prayer specifically to the African American church or community (36–37). In all three of these cases, the scriptural references feel like quotations; none have the orality and musicality that characterize Stewart's prayers, and little of the overall vision of the use of scripture to encode and explicate the historical and social situation of African Americans.

Beginning with Jarena Lee's "Prayer for Sanctification"—which may date from 1808, though it was not published until her spiritual narrative in 1836, one year after Stewart's *Productions*—many of the prayers are heavily narrativized or embedded in narratives for which the prayer serves more as an event than as an independent composition.[14] At the end of Lee's account of her prayer for sanctification—a prayer that, according to Lee, was immediately and dramatically answered—Lee writes, "There is no language that can describe it [the experience of sanctification] except that which was heard by St. Paul, when he is caught to the third heaven, and heard words that it was not lawful to utter" (referencing 2 Corinthians 12:2). In other words, Lee uses a scriptural reference here to draw a veil over the entire experience, a privatized notion of prayer completely foreign to Stewart's very public notion of the prayer genre.

Another common feature of the language of prayer by contemporaries of Stewart is the use of the political language of the day and the discourse of Jeffersonian democracy within the preview of a petition addressed to God. Peter Williams Jr., a sermonizer famous for his published oration on the occasion of the abolition of the slave trade in 1808, prays "for Africa's Children" using the political rhetoric of revolution. He writes of the "deadly arrow of injustice," refers to "the sons of '76," and quotes from the Declaration of Independence (16). Finally, Williams uses the emblematic language made popular in antislavery iconography: "Am I not a man and a brother?" The polar opposite of Lee's highly privatized notion of prayer "within the veil" of the literary text, Williams's acute awareness of the public nature of his written prayer discourse seems to be addressed to the reader/listener more than to God (or to position the listener/reader as the real "God" to whom Williams would appeal for liberation).

Daniel Coker's prayers, culled from his journals, are, like Lee's, heavily embedded within the narrative of the journal itself. Coker's most conspicuous reference is to Moses and the Exodus story, without a doubt the most prominent urtext of African American discourse from the Bible.[15] In one instance, Coker writes: "May he that was with Moses in the wilderness, be with us" (22–23). In another entry, Coker's biblical allusion forms a versified series of interrogatives:

> When will Jehovah hear our cries?
> When will the sun of freedom rise?
> When will for us a Moses stand?
> And bring us out of Pharaoh's hand? (23)

Stewart's role model and direct predecessor David Walker also composed a versified prayer as a part of the third edition of his *Appeal* (1829). Aside from the opening two lines addressed to "thou Alpha and Omega? / The Beginning and the end" (referencing Jesus's self-inscription at the beginning of Revelation), there is little in the way of biblical imagery or language in this text. In the inflammatory racial rhetoric that resulted in censorship by the U.S. mail authorities, who tried to prevent the *Appeal* from falling into southern slave hands, the headnote for the prayer reads "O! save us, we pray thee, thou God of Heaven and of earth, from the devouring hands of the white Christians!!!" (25)

While Stewart does not use such overtly racial language in her own prayers and meditations, she does appeal to a God whom she views as partisan and on the side of African Americans in their struggle for racial equality. Stewart depicts this by portraying African Americans as the "chosen people" of biblical covenant history in the Old Testament, within a comprehensive vision that far extends the Exodus typology to encompass the entire biblical canon.

PERFORMING REVELATIONS

Stewart's prayers and meditations differ from others in this lineage because of her appropriation of scripture to herself. That is, she does not merely quote the Word of God, but rather she speaks it forth as one who has internalized the Bible and made it uniquely her own. Stewart's bold re-voicing of scripture gestures toward a transgression of the prohibition against women "taking a text" or preaching from the Bible in the pulpit, linking her to other female preachers of her era. As Richardson notes, her audience was not always appreciative of such a project, "struggling" as they must have been "with the propriety of encouraging a woman who had appropriated the patriarchal voice of the language of the King James Bible to publicly express her view from a speaker's platform" (16).

While examples of sampling scripture can be found in all the genres of Stewart's writings, I will focus primarily on her use of this technique in the genre of prayer. There are seven prayers interspersed through fourteen meditations, while another prayer is embedded within her religious treatise, *Religion and the Pure Principles of Morality*, which I will treat below. I have prepared an appendix charting all of Stewart's prayers in their order of appearance in *Meditations*; I have labeled these prayers A–G for ease of identification. I have broken each into sections and identified briefly the scriptural reference(s), genre and/or context for the scripture, and, where I felt it was necessary, the entire biblical text for purposes of comparison with Stewart's prayer. I include this detailed close reading in order to demonstrate both the depth and range of Stewart's use of the Bible.

Interestingly, the prose introduction to *Meditations* includes a fine example of intertextual sampling, as Stewart writes, "Though I am sensible that Paul may plant and Apollos water, but that God alone giveth the increase, through Christ strengthening me I can do all things; but that God alone giveth the increase, through Christ strengthening me I can do all things; without him I can do nothing" (24). Out of thirty-three words in this sentence, twenty-six are sampled directly from three separate Bible verses. In order to demonstrate this pattern, it is necessary to break the sentence down into sampled phrases that create their own rhythm and poetic cadence:

> Though I am sensible that Paul may plant, and Apollos water, but that
> God alone giveth the increase,
>   [1 Corinthians 3:16—NT Epistle]
> through Christ strengthening me I can do all things;
>   [Philippians 4:13—NT Epistle, with chiasmic inversion]
> without him I can do nothing.
>   [John 15:5—NT Gospel—words of Jesus]

In this sentence, all of the biblical references are taken from the New Testament, two from epistles and one from the Gospel of John. The first phrase comes from Paul's first letter to the Corinthians, a letter sent to soothe divisions and fractures in the Corinthian church. This is significant because Stewart will regularly pray for "the church to which I belong" in words that suggest difficulty and strife. The phrase taken from Philippians—"I can do all things through Christ who strengtheneth me"—appropriates the words of St. Paul, by chiasmic reversal of their structure. In the final phrase, Stewart samples from the words of Jesus in the self-parable of the true vine in John 15 by inserting her own first person "I" into the utterance.

Another example of this biblical sampling occurs in prayer A, which appears after meditation II. The first line reads: "O thou King eternal, immortal, invisible, and only wise God, before whom angels bow and seraphs veil their faces, crying, holy, holy, holy, holy, is the Lord Almighty" (27). In this one address to God, Stewart has sampled from 1 Timothy 1:17 ("Now unto the King eternal, immortal, invisible, the only wise God") and from a fusion of Isaiah 6:2–3 and Revelation 4:8:

> Isaiah 6:2–3—"Above it stood the seraphims: each had six wings; with twain he covered his face, and with twain he covered his feet, and with twain he did fly.
> And one cried unto another, and said, Holy, holy, holy, is the Lord of hosts: the Whole earth is full of his glory."
>
> Revelation 4:8—"And the four beasts had each of them six wings about him; and they were full of eyes within: and they rest not day and night, saying, Holy, holy, holy, Lord God Almighty, which was, and is, and is to come."

Thus, Stewart has ranged from New Testament pastoral epistle, to Old Testament prophecy, and finally to New Testament apocalypse, all in the invocation of God. This signals the reader that the God that Stewart would address is the God of the entire biblical canon, a gesture that calls forth millennia of history in the interworkings of human with divine in one sweeping gesture of divine naming. Stewart's ability to string together disparate biblical texts within a short, condensed phrase is what I am calling the technique of sampling scripture.

Another fine example of this interweaving occurs in prayer F:

> May the rich be rich in faith and good words towards our Lord Jesus Christ,
>   [1 Timothy 6:18—NT Epistle]
> and may the poor have an inheritance among the saints in light,
>   [James 2:5—NT Epistle]
> a crown incorruptible [1 Corinthians 9:25—NT Epistle]
> that fadeth not away [1 Peter 1:4—NT Epistle]
> eternal in the heavens. [2 Corinthians 5:1—NT Epistle]

In this one sentence, Stewart has combined exhortations to the rich to do good works from 1 Timothy; encouragement to the poor reminding them of their inheritance in God from James; Paul's trope of Greek Olympic runners and the Christian hope of obtaining an "incorruptible crown" in 1 Corinthians; Peter's grand laudatory praise of God, whose inheritance "fadeth not away," in 1 Peter; and Paul's meditation on resurrection and eternal life, which tropes the body as a house or tabernacle, in 2 Corinthians. The train of thought here is interesting. The New Testament that Stewart reconstructs for us speaks to "them that are rich in this world, that they be not highminded," but "that they do good, that they be rich in good works, ready to distribute" (1 Timothy 6:7–8) and to "the poor of this world rich in faith," whom God has chosen to be "heirs of the kingdom" (James 2:5). Her mention of the poor calls to mind passages about future rewards in heaven; thus, Paul's "incorruptible crown" is summoned along with its attendant trope of competitive racing:

> Know ye not that they run in a race run all, but one receiveth the prize? So run, that ye may obtain. And every man that striveth for the mastery is temperate in all things. Now they do it to obtain a corruptible crown; but we an incorruptible. (1 Corinthians 9:24–25)

This phrase, in turn, links up with the eulogistic praise of 1 Peter 1:3–4:

> Blessed be the God and Father of our Lord Jesus Christ, which according to his abundant mercy hath begotten us again unto a lively hope by the resurrection of Jesus Christ from the dead, to an inheritance incorruptible, and undefiled, and that fadeth not away, reserved in heaven for you.

All of these concepts of divine retribution, social leveling, resurrection, and eternity climax as Stewart samples from 2 Corinthians 5:1: "For we know that if our earthly house of this tabernacle were dissolved, we have a building of God, a house not made with hands, eternal in the heavens."

I am suggesting, then, that there is a kind of logic to Stewart's patchwork, a stitching together that goes beyond "proof-texting" as Stewart links scriptures that are tonally resonant with each other around certain themes: her dependence upon God in the face of community divisions in the introduction to *Meditations*; the expansive vision of God as sovereign ruler in the invocation to prayer A; the theme of economic equality and heavenly rewards in prayer F.

The interweaving of meditations, prayers, essays, and speeches occurs in Stewart's most famous work, *Religion and the Pure Principles of Morality, The Sure Foundation on Which We Must Build*. Peterson and Moody read *Religion* correctly, I think, as Stewart's unique expression of the black Jeremiad tradition (see Peterson 66–71; Moody 26–50). Both scholars have also done an excellent job of placing Stewart's prayers and meditations in context and documenting key biblical material in Stewart's repertoire. What I aim to do, then, is to read the relationship between the embedded prayer/poem and the text of *Religion*, as well as to analyze more specifically the pattern of biblical sampling. In other words, I am interested in both the internal intertextuality at work here and the intertextuality between the prayer as "sampling scripture" and the biblical canon. In particular, Stewart's embedding of this prayer within a political/religious essay extends the African American appropriation of the Exodus typology by mapping the entire Old Testament covenant history onto the socio-historical situation of pre-Emancipation African Americans.

I have taken the prayer out of its original printing in prose in order to show how the shift between biblical sampled phrases creates a rhythmic pattern that recalls the tradition of prayer-poems that James Weldon Johnson describes and reinvents in *God's Trombones*. In brackets I have included the scriptural reference and biblical genre of passages that are direct quotations or close paraphrases of actual biblical texts. Where other contexts are helpful or where I feel the reader needs a full text of the actual biblical quotation, I have included these as well. The prayer reads:

> O, Lord God, [first use of this address for God is in Genesis 2:4–3:24]
> the watchmen of Zion [Isaiah 52:8, 62:6; Jeremiah 6:17, 31:6—OT Prophets]
> have cried peace, peace, when there was no peace; [Jeremiah 6:14, 8:12—OT Prophets]
> they have been, as it were, blind leaders of the blind. [Matthew 15:14—NT Gospels—words of Jesus (context: hypocrisy of the Pharisees)]
> Wherefore hast thou so long withheld from us the divine influences of the Holy Spirit?
> Wherefore hast thou hardened our hearts and blinded our eyes [Exodus—7:13, 14; 8:15, 19, 32; 9:7, 12, 34, 35; 14:8 (and other references to God's hardening of Pharaoh's heart)—OT Pentateuch; Isaiah 6:9–10—OT Prophets; Matthew 13:13–17—NT Parables of Jesus; 2 Corinthians 4:4 ("In whom the god of this world hath blinded the minds of Them which believe not, lest the light of the glorious gospel of Christ, who is the Image of God, should shine unto them.")—NT Epistle]
> It is because we have honored thee without lips, when our hearts were far from thee. [Isaiah 29:13—NT Prophets; Matthew 15:8 and Mark 7:6—NT Synoptic Gospels, words of Jesus]
> We have polluted thy Sabbaths, [Ezekiel 20:13, 16, 21, 24—OT Prophets]
> and even our most holy things [Ezekiel 42:13—OT Prophets; echoes Exodus 26:33, 34; 29:37; 30:10, 29:36, and 40:10—OT Pentateuch (references to the building of the tabernacle) and thirteen mentions in the Book of Leviticus (2:3, 10; 6:17, 25, 29; 7:1, 6; 10:12, 17; 14:13; 21:22; 24:9, and 27:28)—OT Pentateuch/Torah]
> have been solemn mockery to thee.
> We have regarded iniquity in our hearts, therefore thou wilt not hear. [Psalm 66:18: "If I regard iniquity in my heart, the Lord will not hear me"—OT Poetry]
> Return again unto us, O Lord God, we beseech thee [Psalms 80:14: "Return, we Beseech thee, O God of hosts"—NT Poetry]

and pardon this the iniquity of thy servants. [Numbers 14:19: "Pardon, I beseech thee, the iniquity of this people"—OT Pentateuch; echoes Exodus 34:9 and Psalm 25:11]

Cause thy face to shine upon us, and we shall be saved. [Psalm 80:3: "Turn us again, O God, and cause thy face to shine; and we shall be saved" (also verses 7 and 19 of a nineteen verse psalm, acts as a refrain); echoes Numbers 6:24-26: "The LORD bless thee, and keep thee: The LORD make his face shine upon thee, and be gracious unto thee: The LORD lift up his countenance upon thee, and give thee peace."—OT Pentateuch; Psalms 67:1: "God be merciful unto us, and bless us; and cause his face to shine upon us"; Psalms 119:135—OT Poetry; and Daniel 9:17—OT Apocalyptic]

O visit us with thy salvation. [Psalms 106:4: "Remember me, O Lord, with the favour that thou bearest unto thy people: O visit me with thy salvation"—OT Poetry]

Raise up sons and daughters unto Abraham [Matthew 3:9: "God is able, of these stones to raise up children unto Abraham"—NT Gospel, words of John the Baptist]

and grant that there might come a mighty shaking of dry bones among us [Ezekiel 37:1-14—OT Prophets]

and a great in-gathering of souls. [Exodus 23:16, 34:22—harvest feasts]

Quicken thy professing children.

Grant that the young may be constrained to believe that there is a reality in religion, and a beauty in the fear of the Lord.

Have mercy on the benighted sons and daughters of Africa.

Grant that we may soon become so distinguished for our moral and religious improvements,

that the nations of the earth may take knowledge of us;

and grant that our cries may come up before thy throne like holy incense [Exodus 31:8 (altar of incense); and Revelation 8:3, 4—NT Apocalypse]

Grant that every daughter of Africa may consecrate her sons to thee from birth.

And do thou, Lord, bestow upon them wise and understanding hearts [Proverbs and wisdom literature].

Clothe us with humility of soul, [1 Peter 5:5—NT Epistle]

and give us a becoming dignity of manners:

may we imitate the character of the meek and lowly Jesus;

and do thou grant that Ethiopia may soon stretch forth her hands unto thee. [Psalms 68:31: "Princes shall come out of Egypt: Ethiopia shall soon stretch out her hands unto God"]

And now, Lord, be pleased to grant that Satan's kingdom may be destroyed; that the kingdom of our Lord Jesus Christ may be built up; that all nations, and kindreds, and tongues, and peoples [Revelation 5:9, 7:9, 14:6—NT Apocalypse]

might be brought to the knowledge of truth, [1 Timothy 2:4—NT Epistle]
as it is in Jesus,
and we at last meet around thy throne, and join in celebrating thy praises. [Revelation 7:9–12, reprise]

By now, what I have been calling the sweeping range of biblical allusion in Stewart's prayers should be evident. In this one prayer she literally takes us from Genesis—with the address "LORD God," distinctive in its first mention in Genesis 2:4–3:24, the beginning of the Yahwistic account of creation, which includes the fall of humanity in the Garden—to Revelation, as she ends by reprising the great meeting around the throne of heaven in the New Testament Apocalypse. Moreover, Stewart's use of the prayer genre embedded in the political essay achieves an act of translation, so to speak, transforming a vertical axis of the relationship between human and divine into a horizontal axis of social analysis.

The problem of agency is a problem invariably raised by Stewart's writings, and it is often linked to the problematic underlying much "uplift" ideology, of which Stewart's writings form an early example.[16] Carla Peterson writes, "In the true tradition of the jeremiad, Stewart's invectives are directed above all against her own people and the destructive ways in which they have reacted to such oppressive conditions, thus intensifying and perpetuating their own degradation" (70). Like David Walker's *Appeal*, with which Stewart was intimately familiar, Stewart's writings "constitute invectives directed *primarily* against her own people rather than her people's oppressors; moreover, blame of her oppressor's brutality is balanced by praise of the literary and scientific culture that they have created for themselves" (66). Yet Peterson points out that, unlike Walker, Stewart focuses more specifically on the question of agency. This meditation on the problem of agency is a direct result of Stewart's familiarity with the Bible. Indeed, the problematic of free will and divine omnipotence that plagues the divine/human relationship forms a major subtext of the English canon of the Bible. That Stewart begins this prayer by signaling the black Jeremiad tradition immediately positions us in the middle of this theoretical/theological dilemma. A focus solely on this literary appropriation of a biblical genre, however, fails adequately to voice the complexity of Stewart's negotiation, since she samples not only from Jeremiah but from a number of biblical prophets and other texts as well. Indeed, other quotations from the prophets (especially from Isaiah) are double-voiced, in that they are also quoted within the New Testament, further developing the problem of agency into the problem of law and grace.

To begin with, the choice of "Lord God" for the initial address to God, among a myriad of other biblical and traditional choices, plants us squarely in the Yahwistic account of the creation and fall in Genesis 2:4–3:24.[17] By sampling the name of God associated with creation, the gendering of humanity, transgression, and the brokenness of the divine/human relationship, Stewart signals the metathemes that will reverberate throughout the prayer. The interconnectedness between the divine/human relationship and relationships that exist between human beings is taken for granted by biblical writers. Thus, problems in the social sphere are already connected to an initial breech of communication between God and humanity.

The phrase "sons and daughters unto Abraham" reverberates in the prayer with a later phrase not sampled from the Bible but from African American literary predecessors like Wheatley and Hammon: "Have mercy on the benighted sons and daughters of Africa." Further, there is another striking phrase: "grant that we may soon become so distinguished for our moral and religious improvements, that the nations of the earth may take knowledge of us" (compare Genesis chapters 12 and 15). Here again, in the form of petition, Stewart is mapping African American collective identity onto the entire covenant history of biblical Israel—expanding the Exodus typology simultaneously backward to the Abraham covenant and forward to the post-exilic cry of the prophets. Later in the prayer there is a biblical petition paraphrased from 1 Peter 5:5: "clothe us with humility of soul" is juxtaposed with a more secular/social concern, "give us a becoming dignity of manners," and summed up with "may we imitate the character of the meek and lowly Jesus" (Matthew 11:28–31) as spiritual, social/temporal, and moral/religious identities become conflated. Like God, who is able from "these stones to raise up children unto Abraham," Stewart has discursively transformed the "benighted sons and daughters of Africa" into the covenant people of the Bible.

Another section of the Bible sampled by Stewart that resonates strongly with African American cultural tradition is Stewart's petition that God "grant that there might come a mighty shaking of dry bones among us," taken from Ezekiel 37:1–14. Johnson writes in *God's Trombones*: "I remember hearing in my boyhood sermons that were current, sermons passed with only slight modifications from preacher to preacher and from locality to locality. Such sermons [included] "The Valley of Dry Bones" which was based on the vision of the prophet in the 37th chapter of Ezekiel" (1). Stewart would certainly gravitate to this story of resurrecting an entire people's dry bones.

Finally, with the phrase "and grant that our cries may come up before thy throne like holy incense," Stewart recalls the altar of incense where the priests offered prayers in the Old Testament Tabernacle and Temple (Exodus 31:8); this is recalled in Revelation as the prayers of the saints coming up before the throne of God (Revelation 8:3–4). Here Stewart reprises Revelation, with visions of the Beloved Community where "all nations, and kindreds, and tongues, and peoples" gather together around the throne—a vision of a new global and multiracial community.

While other black women writers, especially in the nineteenth century, were intimately familiar with the Christian scriptures, few can match the type of cultural performance of Maria W. Stewart's prayers. From Stewart's sweeping communal and global vision we move to Hannah Crafts's vision of empowered female subjects that transgress the domesticized biblicism of the nineteenth century.

CHAPTER FOUR

hannah's craft

BIBLICAL PASSING IN

THE BONDWOMAN'S NARRATIVE

The 2003 edition of Hannah Crafts's *The Bondwoman's Narrative* opens with editor Henry Louis Gates Jr.'s story of literary intrigue, detailing the discovery, acquisition, and authentication of the text. Much of the evidence of the writer's identity, however, derives from Gates's gleaning of internal evidence that links Crafts's story and narrative with actual historical personages, places, and events, as well as with much of what we already know about pre-Emancipation African American writing and textual practices. The debate about the racial identity of Crafts continues. While some reviewers surmise that Crafts is a white woman writing an "ethnic impersonator" narrative, others maintain that she is black. Adebayo Williams says, for example, "This novel could not have been conceived and written by a white person, except by a ventriloquist and sadomasochist of impossible genius" (10).[1]

Not only is authorship problematic in *The Bondwoman's Narrative*, but genre is difficult as well. Like *Autobiography of an Ex-Colored Man*, first published anonymously in 1912 and later published as a novel by James Weldon Johnson, with *The Bondwoman's Narrative* we may be dealing with a text that is *passing* on several levels.[2] Indeed, Hannah's *craft* as a writer is evident in the demands her narrative places on the reader to attend to the interweaving of the historical, tropological, and hermeneutical registers of its intertextuality. Crafts's novel clearly functions outside the usual abolitionist formula for slave narratives or antislavery novels, as John Stauffer points out. As Adebayo Williams suggests, "There was no way the manuscript could have found accommodation in the literary politics of antebellum America" (3). Williams concludes:

> the black community and the abolitionists would have been scandalized by
> the brutal and frank portrayal of slave life and the social condescensions of the
> author.... At the other extreme of the political spectrum, the proslave lobby
> would have been taken aback by the shrill ferocity of the book's denunciation of

slavery . . . as well as by the nettling social commentary. . . . Like all original artists, Hannah Crafts was true to herself. But the price for such unsettling originality and adamantine integrity is significant exclusion. (3)

Lawrence Buell also comments on "the unabashed nature of the fictionalization" of the narrative, in an era obsessed with African American truth-telling and authentication" ("Bondwoman Unbound" 19). From the beginning of the text, Crafts sounds a different note; the narrative demonstrates a *spiritual authenticity* that may account for our difficulties in affixing racial certainty to its narrative voice. While readers of the narrative have linked her use of the Bible to the narratives of Hagar in Genesis 16 and 21, Hannah in 1 Samuel, and Jacob and Esau (also in Genesis), scholars have missed the profound use of subtext and misdirection that the narrative encodes. It is a narrative predicated on making the reader expect the unexpected.

Whether or not Hannah Crafts is ever identified beyond the shadow of a doubt, the narrative does bear certain signatures that link it with the lineage of black women's textuality, especially black women's biblicism and the development of an antislavery hermeneutic through narrative and fiction. Crafts's consistent use of scriptural verses to begin each chapter and of internal soundings and biblical echoes is not merely decorative or pious but form part of a comprehensive Judeo-Christian worldview. Bryan Sinche argues that Crafts attempts to "construct a story that validates the God who presides over the peculiar institution, while still condemning the institution itself" (175–76). Moreover, he writes, "by adhering to a strict conception of Christian virtue that many slave authors would deem incompatible with resistance to slavery, Hannah follows a different path toward rebellion" (176). I would go so far as to say that the key to interpreting this text—and the most consistent element of *The Bondwoman's Narrative*—is the certainty of a moral universe grounded in Crafts's belief in the supernatural as an active agent in the lives of her characters.

Beginning each chapter with a verse of scripture renders her text a literary pulpit, as she boldly "takes a text" along with other black women preachers like Jarena Lee, Zilpha Elaw, and Amanda Berry Smith, who challenged prohibitions against black female preaching. Writing of Crafts's "heterodox scriptural imagination" ("Bondwoman Unbound" 19), Lawrence Buell notes that she "was capable of invoking the antebellum period's most important literary master text [the Bible]" (17). Buell sums up the artistry of Crafts's biblical style as follows:

> This was an author who, despite facing obvious impediments to the mastery of the dominant high culture, was capable of invoking the antebellum period's most

important literary master text with a subtlety—at best—equal to the classics of high canonical Anglo-American literary scripturism by Emerson, Dickinson, Hawthorne, Melville, Stowe, and others. The Bible was by far the best-selling, most accessible, most cited book in the United States between the Revolution and the Civil War; and Hannah Crafts, an eager if not encyclopedic reader, showed herself as adept in creative hermeneutics as any of the authors aforesaid. (17)

For Buell, Crafts's connections to the Bible involve a kind of punning with her name, saying that the "H" in Hannah Crafts's (possibly pseudonymous) name "can only mean Hagar . . . a common name for female slaves as well as a popular, complexly symbolic figure in nineteenth-century literature and art" (16). Buell goes on to note that in naming herself Hannah instead of Hagar, Crafts creates a "double-helix constellation of H's" by referencing not one but two biblical women: Hagar and Hannah.

Augusta Rohrbach comments on Crafts's embedding of the Genesis story of Jacob and Esau in her novel, arguing that "her narrative itself corresponds loosely to his story in Genesis" (65):

> Jacob becomes a symbol of freedom in Crafts's story; his presence—in the pages of her Bible and as a character in her novel—facilitates her safe journey to the promised land. . . . His death in the novel, as in Genesis, paves the way to the land of freedom—the North for Crafts, Israel for Jacob, which is also the name God gives Jacob. (66)

Others have commented on the figure of Mrs. Henry as the ideal white Christian woman and a prototype of the "virtuous woman" of Proverbs 31, which Crafts uses for an epigraph (Bruce). While all of these readings have merit, I would like to focus this chapter on Crafts's references to the Shulamite trope of *Song of Songs*, to which she adds brilliantly the story of Esther as a narrative of passing, and the passion narrative that underwrites black women's Christology. These biblical figures come into play with the introduction of the new mistress and the intrigue surrounding her racial identity, not unlike the mystery of the writer's own racial identity. In telling this story of the mysterious new mistress, Crafts also uses language that recalls the nineteenth-century fascination with the Queen of Sheba as an emblem of womanly wisdom and power. Through all of these biblical echoes, Crafts skillfully dismantles ideologies of race, gender, and color in her text.

BIBLICAL PASSING AND BLACK WOMEN'S SUBJECTIVITY

> I have said that I always had a quiet way of observing things, and this habit grew upon me, sharpened perhaps by the absence of all elemental knowledge. Instead of books I studied faces and characters, and arrived at conclusions by a sort of sagacity that closely approximated to the unerring of animal instinct.
>
> Hannah Crafts, *The Bondwoman's Narrative*

Since the character Hannah—and perhaps the author as well—is a minister's wife at the end of the *Bondwoman's Narrative*, it is significant that the narrator consistently "takes a text," encoding each chapter as a type of black women's sermonic discourse. In this sense, each chapter involves taking a biblical text, both as illustration and exposition. Chapter one opens with a quotation from the *Song of Songs*, featuring the Shulamite trope that I have been able to locate as early as Zilpha Elaw's 1846 *Memoirs*.[3] Crafts exploits, in a more overt way, the double-vision of the gaze by citing verse 6a from the first chapter of the *Song*—"look not upon me, because I am black, the sun hath looked upon me"—rather than the usual verse 5—"I am black but comely." The play of language of sight here ("look not upon me . . . the sun hath looked upon me") simultaneously invites and repels the reader's gaze, inhabiting both parts of the "but/and" dichotomy that frames the discourse of the Shulamite figure since the patristic and late medieval periods. More importantly, it represents the double bind of black female sexuality and desire.[4] This linguistic doubling is extended to the actual text when Crafts writes:

> No one ever spoke of my father or mother, but I soon learned what a curse was attached to my race, soon learned that the African blood in my veins would forever exclude me from the higher walks of life. That toil unremitted unpaid toil must be my lot and portion, without even the hope or expectation of any thing better. This seemed the harder to be borne, because my complexion was almost white, and the obnoxious descent could not be readily traced, though it gave a rotundity to my person, a wave and curl to my hair, and perhaps led me to fancy pictorial illustrations and flaming colors. (5–6)

Interestingly enough, this breaking of the visual field of race and searching for alternative signifiers would become important to the passing narrative of the postreconstruction and Harlem Renaissance periods in Johnson's *Autobiography of an Ex-Colored Man*, the DuBois essay "On the Passing of the First Born" in *Souls of Black Folk*, and Jessie Fauset's novel *Plum Bun*. Similarly, Crafts seeks simultaneously to establish and to deconstruct the racial code of the time by exposing the fallacy that race is based on discernible difference in skin color; instead, blackness is a function of invisible "African blood" in spite of a "complexion . . . almost white." The displacement of race as visual difference is represented in subtle markers such as "rotundity," "wave and curl" to the hair, and even preferences for "pictorial illustrations and flaming color." This breaking of the visual markers of racial difference prefigures the passing novel and exposes the concept of race as the ultimate fiction.

The phrase that stands out in the context of this study, however, is the language of race as a "curse," especially as it is contrasted with the use of the term in the preface to *Bondwoman's Narrative*: "Have I succeeded in portraying any of the peculiar features of that institution whose curse rests over the fairest land the sun shines upon? Have I succeeded in showing how it blights the happiness of the white as well as the black race?" (3) The language of slavery as a "curse" and "blight" is held in tension with the statement in chapter one that race (read: blackness, Africanness) is the curse. In the preface, Crafts suggests that the real curse is not blackness per se but slavery. In this sense, she deconstructs race by framing the curse of slavery within a nationalistic concept of America as "the fairest land the sun shines upon." The "whitening" of America here is important because the reference to the sun invokes the epigraph to chapter one from *Song of Songs*: "the sun hath looked upon [blackened] me." In other words, Crafts is arguing that slavery "blackens" the very notion of America as "the fairest land." This could refer to a metaphoric, moral failure and literally to miscegenation and the rape of black women slaves whose offspring literally changed the complexion of the land. In the juxtaposition of these two passages, America becomes identified with the character of Hannah herself: as she is "cursed" with blackness, America is cursed and "blighted" by slavery. In this sense, America (made up of blacks and whites) becomes the Shulamite of the *Song of Songs*. By extension, black enslaved women are the ultimate trope for America itself, the prototypical native *daughters*—produced by America and, through the legal discourse of *partus sequitur ventrem*—who in turn are the producers of an America literally and figuratively blackened through the institution of slavery. Crafts, in casting a shadow on the very idea of America, deflects the gaze of specularity away from her own body onto the body politic via a redirection of racial discourse. The myth of a "white" America is the ultimate passing narrative.

The shifting shadows of racial ideology that play across the color line continue with the introduction of the passing narrative via the bridal plot, which begins rather abruptly early on. The entrance of the bridal plot continues the theme invoked by the Shulamite trope, since the history of the interpretation of the biblical *Song of Songs* revolves around courtship and what Ricoeur calls the "nuptial metaphor."[5] Within chapter two is a phrase that gives a subtle clue to the crossing of the marriage and passing plots in the text: "Sir Clifford made it a boast that he never retracted, that his commands and decisions like *the laws of the Medes and Persians* were inalterable and so he bade her rise and do his bidding at once, of that in case of refusal he should enforce her obedience by a punishment of which she had no ~~conception~~ [sic] idea" (22, my emphasis). Embedded within this statement of the master's autocratic power is a phrase that readers familiar with the Bible would recognize as coming from the Old Testament post-exhilic Book of Esther, which features a Jewish girl's sudden social elevation to queen, predicated on her keeping silent about her racial identity.[6] Esther's rise to power follows the departure of Vashti, the first wife of Ahasuerus (or Xerxes, as his name is rendered in some translations), who is banished from the palace because she refuses to dance before Ahsuerus's party guests. Memucan, one of the king's advisers, sums up the implications of Vashti's feminist defiance before Ahasuerus and the other princes and urges the king to act:

> Vashti the queen hath not done wrong to the king only, but also to all the princes, and to all the people that are in all the provinces of the king Ahasuerus. For this deed of the queen shall come abroad unto all women, so that they shall despise their husbands in their eyes, when it shall be reported. . . . If it please the king, let there go a royal commandment from him, and let it be written among *the laws of the Persians and the Medes, that it be not altered* that Vashti come no more before king Ahasuerus; and let the king give her royal estate unto another that is better than she. (Esther 1:16–19, my emphasis)

The search for a replacement for Vashti ends in the selection of Esther, a young Jewish girl (originally named Hadassah), who is advised by her uncle and guardian Mordecai to conceal her heritage: "Esther had not shown her people nor her kindred: for Mordecai had charged her that she should not show it" (Esther 2:10).

In "Feminist Providence," Joyce Zonana traces the interest in Esther in the nineteenth century by writers like Charlotte Bronte and Tennyson, uncovering a feminist hermeneutic that refuses readings by Bible commentators that insist on the split between a disobedient Vashti and a compliant Esther. In contrast, women like Eliza Cushing, Frances Harper, Harriet Beecher Stowe, and Elizabeth Cady Stanton, Zonana argues, read Vashti's refusal as "dutiful disobedience" and took a decidedly feminist stance, even going so far as to read Esther as disobedient and defiant rather than submissive. "The relationship between Vashti's rebellion and Esther's triumph are central to understanding Charlotte Bronte's *Jane Eyre* and *Villette*" (240). During the Harlem Renaissance, poet Anne Spencer referenced Vashti in her poem "Before the Feast of Shushan."

The poem is a mock-dialogue and, having been summoned by the king, Vashti muses:

> And I am hard to force the petals wide;
> And you are fast to suffer and be sad.
> Is any prophet come to teach a new thing
> Now in a more apt time?

The poem ends with the demanding words of the king:

> I, thy lord, like not manna for meat as a Judahn;
> I, thy master, drink, and red wine, plenty, and when
> I thirst. Eat meat, and full, when I hunger.
> I, thy King, teach you and leave you, when I list.
> No woman in all Persia sets out strange action
> To confuse Persia's lord—
> Love is but desire and thy purpose fulfillment;
> I, thy King, so say![7]

The poem breaks off just before Vashti's subversive act, positioning the reader as coconspirator to her actions.

The genius of Crafts's appropriation of Esther is that she perceives the story as fundamentally a passing narrative and adds the dimension of race to this feminist hermeneutic by specifically combining the passing and marriage plots. In *The Bondswoman's Narrative*, one of the epigraphs is from the book of Esther: "We were sold for nought, I and my people" (chapter 16, 195). This strategy of introducing a subtext by foreshadowing—and then displacing it onto a later section of the novel—is typical of Crafts. Early in the novel she drops hints of the later unfolding of the marriage/passing narrative by referring to "the daughter of a queen" (8) and "his beautiful bride" (13). She also writes that "the pale pure features of a bride descend in a halo of glory" (16). A syntactical equivalence develops early between bride, queen, and paleness or fairness. In weaving together the passing and bridal plots, Crafts conflates the story of Esther with the figure of another popular nineteenth-century biblical woman, the Queen of Sheba, often thought to be a possible suitor or bride of King Solomon.[8]

QUEEN FOR A DAY: THE QUEEN OF SHEBA AND RACIAL IDENTITY

The Queen of Sheba is associated with Solomon in the Old Testament (1 Kings 19:1–13; 2 Chronicles 9:1–12) and stands at the center of a number of interrelated racial and gendered representations. Unlike Esther, who in the nineteenth century is always portrayed as white, the Queen of Sheba is historically depicted as black. In at least two artistic renderings, she is portrayed alongside both Solomon and Balaam. Biblical scholars disagree on the real origins of the Queen of Sheba. Just as the Shulamite is associated with a variety of biblical women, from Moses's Cushite wife to the maiden given to comfort an aging King David (1 Kings 1:2–4) to an Egyptian princess, the Queen of Sheba "has been regarded as reigning over regions embracing lands from India to Ethiopia" (Copher 158). The debate centers on whether to associate her with southwest Asia or the continent of Africa, a detail of great interest to those assessing "the black presence" in the Bible. Cain Hope Felder, for example, following Origen and Jerome, claims decisively that "the Queen of Sheba was a Cushite, a Black royal personage" (*Troubling Biblical Waters* 13). Edwin Yamauchi, however, tracing the Queen of Sheba in Jewish, Christian, Ethiopian, and Islamic traditions, believes that biblical and archaeological evidence locates the Queen of Sheba's origins "in southwest Arabia" (105). Beyond her racial and national identity, the Queen of Sheba often figured in nineteenth-century discourse as a symbol of wisdom and power.

All of this begins to come into view in *The Bondwoman's Narrative* with the introduction of the new mistress within a cloud of secrecy:

> I was studying her, and making out a mental inventory of her foibles, and weaknesses, and caprices, and whether or not she was likely to prove an indulgent mistress. I did not see, but I felt that there was mystery, something indefinable about her. She was a small brown woman, with a profusion of wavy curly hair, large bright eyes, and delicate features with the exception of her lips which were too large, full, and red. She dressed in very good taste and her manner seemed perfect but for an uncomfortable habit she had of seeming to watch everybody as though she feared them or thought them enemies. (27)

Given the prior description of Hannah herself, the reader is meant to read clues like "a profusion of wavy curly hair" and "lips . . . too large, full, and red" as signifiers of race. The fact that the mistress is shadowed by the black, obscure figure of Trappe, the slave catcher, is a further clue to the reader. The epigraph to the second chapter, titled "The Bride and the Bridal Company," is from "Proverbs of Solomon": "when he speaks fair, believe him not; for there are severe abominations in his heart" (Proverbs 26:25). That this text speaks of concealment, deceit, and "talebear[ing]" (Proverbs 26:22) announces a plot that will turn on misdirection and misrecognition.

Chapter three is appropriately entitled "Progress in Discovery" and begins by disclosing the figure of Mr. Trappe, "the old gentleman in black" (31). Hannah overhears "a conversation designed to be entirely confidential" (39), and the mistress's racial identity is exposed. Unlike Esther, who emerges triumphant within the biblical narrative and who chooses to unveil her true identity in order to save her people from genocide, Hannah's mistress is not in control of the disclosure of her mixed race heritage. Mr. Trappe, unlike the sadistic Haman of Esther's story, is not "entrapped" by his own schemes in a kind of divine retribution, but rather continues to terrorize her with his knowledge of her secret. Thus, the mistress's characterization as Esther evolves into her refiguration as the suffering Christ.

This transfiguration of character creates an interesting progression in the novel through the figure of the passing mistress: from the Shulamite woman/Queen of Sheba, a woman whose significance lies in her attractiveness to King Solomon; to Esther, a queen in her own right; to Jesus, the absolute center of New Testament narrative, crowned in Revelation as "King of Kings and Lord of Lords." One wonders if Crafts's masking of her own authorial identity and displacement of biblical texts stemmed from her nervousness about the irreverence of presenting a female Messiah.[9] The character of the passing mistress is impulsive and emotionally unstable; yet mixed with a stock portrayal of the sentimental heroine are clear references to Christ from the gospel narratives.

The Christological references begin with comments from Trappe and Hannah that position the mistress as a Christ within pericopes of the Woman with the Issue of Blood (Matthew 9:20–21) and the Woman with the Alabaster Box (Luke 7:37–38). Having established her in an elevated position, the narrative evokes the theme of the egalitarian relationship between Jesus and his followers (represented by Hannah) during an exchange where the mistress refuses any socially designated title:

"I will, my dear mistress."

"Call me mistress no longer. Henceforth you shall be to me as a very dear sister" she said embracing me again. "Oh to be free, to be free."

There was something ominous to me in the transports of her joy. Her eyes were illuminated and her countenance shone. The transition was sudden and complete, but it is even thus with impulsive natures.

"My dear Mistress."

"There: there, mistress again when I have forbidden it."

"Well then, my dear friend, let us weigh this matter well." (48)

This scene echoes the words of Christ in a composite evocation of John 13, when he washes the disciples' feet, and John 15, the beginning of the Olivet discourse, in which he issues them his "final instructions" before going to the cross. In chapter 13 of John, Jesus refuses the designations of "master" and "lord" and stoops to the disciples' level, performing the role of the lowest house servant by washing their feet. In chapter 15, he continues in this vein and renames himself the disciples' "friend": "Greater love hath no man than this, that a man lay down his life for his friends. Ye are my friends" (John 15:13-14).

Jesus's divesture of earthly power and hierarchy prefigures the cross in John's gospel, just as Hannah's mistress, in flattening the social distinctions between them, foreshadows her own hideous death. She cries out to Hannah, "Heaven, I fear has turned against us," echoing Jesus's quotation of Psalm 22:1 from the cross, "My God, My God, why has thou forsaken me?" But one of the most curious Christological references involves the mysterious way the mistress dies. In chapter seven, the young woman dies by rupturing a blood vessel, recalling Jesus in the garden of Gethsemane, where he "sweat great drops of blood" (Luke 22:44). Hannah, in a sort of baptism/communion reference, cradles her head and "the blood gushed afresh, staining my hands and clothes" (100). The idea of having one's hands, and clothing, "washed in the blood" is a prevalent biblical trope for salvation and cleansing from sin: from the Levitical law of sprinkling blood of the sacrifice for consecration and cleansing, to the Passover in Exodus, to Revelation's portrait of saints in heaven as those "who had their garments washed and made white in the blood of the Lamb" (Leviticus 4:29-31; Exodus 12:12-13; Revelation 7:13-14). Perhaps more significantly, chapter eight of *The Bondwoman's Narrative* begins, like the chapters that follow the Crucifixion in the gospels, with images of resurrection. First, Hannah claims that "My beloved companion, my idolized mistress I know not where they laid her" (101). The language here harkens back to the idea of the Beloved in *Song of Songs* and the complaint of Mary Magdalene after her discovery of the empty tomb in the gospels. Similarly, Crafts writes of the mistress's death:

> No kind compassionate countenance beamed upon me, no sweet familiar voice greeted my ear, yet weeping, sighing, moaning in utter loneliness I felt in my heart that it was better much better for her. She had escaped wo[e] and oppression, and insult, and degradation. Through death she had conquered her enemy, and rose triumphant above his machinations, and I longed to follow her. (101)

This lament over the one who had been her companion in the wilderness turns on Hannah's awareness of a *méconnaissance*: that Jesus, in the gospels accounts, was Himself a passer, whose true identity—His divinity—is only recognized in death and resurrection. I would not go so far as to argue that Crafts is attempting to portray a female deity or to feminize Jesus. Rather, as a devout Christian and in her desire to portray this character in the most positive, sympathetic light, Crafts can think of no higher compliment than to characterize her, literally and figuratively, as Christ-like. Indeed, in the New Testament, the highest aspiration of any Christian, regardless of gender, is to be "conformed to the image of Christ" (Romans 8:29). Yet within this domesticated evangelicalism lurks a subversive subtext. Hannah's craft has been to transform domesticized images of women into increasingly empowered figures—from Vashti/Esther, who challenges royal authority; to the Queen of Sheba, who is represented as a regal equal of Solomon; to Jesus, the "King of Kings."

> Write the vision
> and make it plain upon tables,
> that he may run that readeth it.
>
> HABAKKUK 2:2–3

> As a writer reading, I came to realize the obvious:
> the subject of the dream is the dreamer.
>
> TONI MORRISON, *Playing in the Dark*

CHAPTER FIVE

"beyond mortal vision"

IDENTIFICATION AND MISCEGENATION IN THE

JOSEPH CYCLE AND HARRIET E. WILSON'S *OUR NIG*

Although the Genesis story of Joseph's enslavement and triumphant rise to power would seem to be directly applicable to African Americans in the eighteenth and nineteenth centuries, scholars differ on the importance of the Joseph cycle to African American writers. Cain Hope Felder asserts in *Troubling Biblical Waters* that "the story of Joseph sold into slavery by his brothers (Gen. 37:1–36) and the great Exodus saga (Exodus, Deuteronomy) have become focal points in the Pentateuch for Blacks" (17); yet Felder only references a small portion of the entire narrative about Joseph, and he offers no example of a single black text that draws its inspiration from Genesis 37. More recently the debate has been framed by Phillip Richards and Allen Dwight Callahan, who differ sharply about the significance and interpretation of Joseph. Richards has called the books of Genesis and Exodus, especially the story of Joseph in Genesis 37–50, the "prototypes for Early Black Anglophone writing," while Callahan argues that "African Americans rarely identified with Joseph" (112).[1] It is important to note that Richards reads the text as fundamentally about "the displaced—by virtue of nationality, race, class or social provenance—hero within the domestic world of the upper-class or aristocratic household of another culture" (223). Callahan, however, views Joseph as a story of upward mobility: "Joseph's boundless confidence and upward mobility, occasional reverses notwithstanding, was so unlike the collective experience of American slaves and their descendants that his story did not speak to their present condition" (112). The meaning of Joseph's plight, then, appears to be in the eyes of the beholders.

The story of Joseph enters the discourse of race and slavery, both through correspondence and negation, sameness and difference. In its earliest appropriation, the Puritan judge Samuel Sewall used the story for the purposes of arguing against the slave trade (*The Selling of Joseph*). In an early example of the "brotherhood of man" ideology, Sewall argued that whites selling Africans into slavery was analogous to Joseph's brothers selling him to the Egyptian slave caravan. Calling enslaved Africans "the Sons of Adam" and (at least potentially) sons (and daughters?) of "the last ADAM" (i.e., Christ), Sewall concludes that "originally, and Naturally, there is no such thing as Slavery."

Sewall's pamphlet ranges over several ideological supports for slavery and the slave trade, including the curse of Ham exegesis and the doctrine of merciful enslavement. His quotation of Ephesians sums up his counter-hermeneutic: "since the partition Wall is broken down, inordinate Self love should likewise be demolished."[2] That his argument is primarily against the slave trade, and only secondarily about slavery in general, is clear from his quotation of the economic Latin phrase, "Caveat Emptor!"

Sewall wrote the pamphlet, among other motives, as part of his defense in the ruling of Adam, a slave who sought freedom from his owner, Judge Saffin. In this "battle of the judges," Saffin directly refutes Sewall's exegesis of the Joseph narrative in *A Brief and Candid Answer to a Late Printed Sheet Entitled The Selling of Joseph*:

THE NEGROES CHARACTER

Cowardly and cruel are those
   Blacks Innate,
Prone to Revenge, Imp of
   inveterate hate
He that exasperates them,
   soon espies
Mischief and Murder in their
   very eyes.
Libidinous, Deceitful, False
   and Rude,
The Spume Issue of Ingratitude.
The Premises consider'd, all
   may tell,
How near good *Joseph* they
   are parallel.

As Sewall sought to forge a link between African Americans and Joseph (and by extension African Americans and Adam/Christ), Saffin's goal is not only to weaken but to destroy the link through the use of racial stereotypes. The use of the word "parallel" in Saffin's verse is interesting, as it resonates with "parable," which in Greek means "to throw alongside." The value of Joseph as a parable for African American identity in narrative depends, it seems, on the value one assigns to disparate elements of the story.

In 1827, David Walker's militant *Appeal in Four Articles* would enact a stunning reversal to Sewall's strategy—but Walker, unlike Saffin, would do so in the cause of antislavery discourse. Arguing that American slavery was fundamentally different from the type of slavery Joseph endured in Egypt, Walker sought to drive a wedge between the biblical text and American chattel slavery. Walker exploited the triumphalist narrative of the successful Joseph in Egypt, which he racializes by claiming that "the Egyptians, were Africans or colored people, such as we are."[3] This supports Walker's overall thesis in the *Appeal* that black Americans are the most "wretched" people ever to suffer under a system of enslavement. Yet the distancing from Joseph, despite his having been a slave, leaves Walker's argument vulnerable, as he later wants to equate the Egyptians, whom he has referred to as "about the same as you see the colored people of the United States at the present day," with white American enslavers.[4]

None of these readings, however, account for gender, nor do they reference African American women writers who found in the Joseph story a voice for their own self-representations. While we might think of obvious women biblical characters like Hagar, the Shulamite, Esther, and others as inspirations for African American women's self-representations, Joseph represents a departure from the identification with female-specific characters. This chapter examines Harriet E. Wilson's 1859 novel *Our Nig* in terms of her use of the Joseph cycle as the vehicle for her own self-fashioning. In this sense, the Joseph story becomes a literal and figurative mask for Wilson as she exposes the problem of gender in the narrative. For Wilson, the Joseph narrative serves as a way of critiquing the "American dream-text" of the "two story white house, North," by exposing the reality of northern racism and de facto slavery. That biblical scholars refer to the concluding chapters of Genesis, 37–50, as the "Joseph Cycle" leads us to expect a cohesive narrative of Joseph's betrayal, enslavement, and ultimate rise to power in Egypt. However, there is a long tradition, derived primarily from the redaction theory of hermeneutics, of treating chapter 38, which depicts the sexual exploitation of Tamar by her father-in-law, Judah, as an interruption or digression to the main plot of the narrative, and thus as a marginalization of gender as a displaced identity. Even in claiming the subversive potential of Tamar's story, David Jobling notes that "Genesis 38 famously intrudes into the Jacob-Joseph story" (131). In her black and female text, Wilson reads/writes at the margins of the biblical text as narratives of women's sexual victimization under slavery, and its northern "shadows" are central to her representations. Unlike earlier readings by both white and black men (e.g., Sewall, Equiano, and Walker), Wilson chose to focus neither on the *selling* of Joseph (chapter 37) nor on the triumphalist ending (chapter 42 and following), but rather on Joseph's time in prison (chapters 40–41), as the prison narrative figures both the prison-house of gendered/racial language and the female imprisonment that thematically connects so many nineteenth-century women's texts.[5] Important for my analysis here, these often elided middle chapters are organized around Joseph's skill as an interpreter of dreams, which harkens back to his original dream in Genesis 37. Thus Wilson's text deconstructs the notion of the "dream" even as it situates the black woman writer as both teller and interpreter of dreams/texts, foregrounding interpretation and hermeneutics.

Gay Gibson Cima's concept of the "host body" is helpful in explaining Wilson's use of a (male) biblical figure to illuminate black female subjectivity. Cima uses the term to designate a "spectral body, a generic body in movement, an abstraction which nonetheless serves as a life-like body shield" (4) for women who ventured onto the male-dominated terrain of public critical performance. In addition to individual performance, Cima theorizes the host body as collective, a site for an imagined community "alongside or outside of nationhood" (5).

Cima states that her conceptualization of the host body is an "amplification" of Joseph Roach's work in theater studies on bodily substitution and "surrogation," in order to account for gender. Thus she posits a term that represents not merely a diachronic displacement, as Roach views surrogation, but one that inhabits a middle ground "between center and margin, material and immaterial" (6). In other words, Cima's take on the host body goes beyond the idea of material substitution and aims to consider ways in which women's discourse and performance reveals a space between body and spirit, between material and spiritual. "Women critics," she writes, "attempted to find a zone in between embodiment and abstraction, a bodily space within which they could safely speak or write, while protecting their material bodies and creating new hermeneutic pathways for perceiving those bodies. I am calling this space the 'host body.' Host bodies resist materialization" (6). An example of this protective rhetorical gesture occurs in the work of Wilson's contemporary, Harriet Jacobs, who used pseudonyms not only for herself as author, but for the entire cast of characters in *Incidents in the Life of a Slave Girl* (1861). Key names are taken from the Joseph cycle, including "Jacobs," which echoes the biblical patriarch whose name means "usurper" in Hebrew. Jacobs indeed represents herself as a usurper or trickster (see the chapter called "A Competition in Cunning") in the text. That her uncle is named Benjamin, the same name as Joseph's younger brother, is another play on Genesis.

Similarly, Jarena Lee's appropriation of the Jonah narrative, when she exclaims "I was like Jonah," protects her from scrutiny and retribution as she interrupts a male preacher's sermon in the following passage:

> I told them that I was like Jonah; for it had been then nearly eight years since the Lord had called me to preach his gospel to the fallen sons and daughters of

Adam's race, but that I had lingered like him, and delayed to go at the bidding of
the Lord, and warn those who are as deeply guilty as were the people of Ninevah.
(*Life and Religious Experience* 44)

This cross-gender identification in black women's texts allows for the assumption of more authority than even the Bible typically affords women by appropriating the prophetic mantle from within the Bible itself.

THE LAW OF THE FATHER/PHARAOH
AND THE AMERICAN RACIAL DREAM-TEXT

Even with the discovery and publication of Hannah Crafts's *The Bondwoman's Narrative* and its accompanying controversy, Harriet E. Wilson's 1859 novel *Our Nig; or, Sketches from the Life of a Free Black* stands as a kind of Genesis story in the African American, black women's, and American literary canons. Unlike Crafts's text, Wilson relates the story of a black girl born in "freedom," and thus it represents a break from the traditional fugitive slave narrative genre, although "slavery's shadows" continue to inform Wilson's relativizing of northern freedom for black and poor women. *Our Nig* tells the story of Frado, a spirited mulatta who, through the death of her black father and the abandonment of her white mother, ends up an indentured servant in the home of a white, middle-class, New England family, the Bellmonts. Wilson's agenda is emphasized in her preface to the novel, as she refers to Mrs. Bellmont, the matriarch, as "wholly imbue with *southern principles*," a characterization central to Wilson's overall project of exposing the northern indenture system as a kind of slavery.[6]

Yet Wilson does not stop at implicating the North in slavery and slavery-like practices; rather, on the metalevel of the text, she skillfully references and dismantles two powerful and pervasive myths of origin that work to mutually construct ideologies of race and gender: the Bible's Genesis and the law of *partus sequitur ventrem*, which stipulates that the slave child follows the condition of the mother. The curse of the black maternal, then, is at the root of black female representation in *Our Nig*, even as Wilson's questioning of the mythography of its power opens the way to (potential) blessing. Structurally, just as Genesis moves from Creation to Eden, the Fall, and the emergence of God's covenant with the people of Israel, ending with the Joseph cycle in chapters 37–50, *Our Nig* begins with a story of creation and "fall"—the saga of "lonely Mag Smith," Frado's mother—and ends, in the very last sentence of the novel proper, with a reference to Joseph:

> But think on me when it shall be well with thee, and show kindness, I pray thee, unto me, and make mention of me unto Pharaoh, and bring me out of this house:

for indeed I was stolen away out of the land of the Hebrews: and here also have I done nothing that they should put me into the dungeon. (Genesis 40:14–15)

After a moment of conventional closure, in which the narrator recounts the destiny of the Bellmont family, a closure that purports to be, as the last chapter promises, "the winding up of the matter," the text reopens, as it were, onto an unfamiliar and *unfamilial* landscape. In a gesture that prefigures Toni Morrison's *Beloved*, Frado becomes *disembodied*; she appears as a "haunt," refiguring the terrain of memory and desire in the novel. Wilson writes: "Frado has disappeared from their [the surviving Bellmonts'] memories, as Joseph from the butler's, but she will never cease to track them till beyond mortal vision" (131). The ambiguity of the phrasing here leaves room for multiple readings. Yet I cannot help but be drawn to the phrase "beyond mortal vision" as a suggestion that there is something beyond the text's visual frame of representation, another kind of vision for which the allusion to the biblical story of Joseph serves as an important lens. Long before Freud's theorizing of the dream as a realm of condensation and displacement, Wilson, through the appropriation of the biblical narrative of Joseph, seems to foreshadow the importance of dreams and dreaming in framing human subjectivity. Indeed, Wilson does not so much anticipate Freud as recover the importance of dreams in biblical narrative, Freud's likely original source of much psychoanalytic theory. Beyond both, however, Wilson examines the sociohistorical efficacy of racial exclusion as the underside of the American dream. By invoking this story of Joseph at the end of *Our Nig*, Wilson positions herself, through the narrator and the main character, Frado, simultaneously within multiple narratives as betrayed kin, slave, prophet, and, significantly, as interpreter of dreams. This multiple self-positioning foregrounds interpretation as a leading figure in the novel's plot and as an important element within its overall structure.

Sold into slavery by his jealous older brothers (Genesis 37), Joseph is jailed by his master, Potiphar, for allegedly raping Potiphar's wife, who has accused Joseph as a result of his having resisted *her* sexual advances (Genesis 39). Chapter 40 opens as two of Pharaoh's servants, the butler and the chief baker, are thrown into jail with Joseph. Both men dream that night and awake the next morning in agony because "there is no interpreter" to assign meaning to their dreams. Claiming that "interpretations belong to God" (Genesis 40:8), Joseph successfully interprets the dreams, and it is at this point that he pleads with the butler, to whom Wilson refers, saying, "think on me when it shall be well with thee.... And make mention of me unto Pharaoh, and bring me out of this house" (Genesis 40:14). Joseph's plea for remembrance is neither sentimental nor spiritual but material and economic, connected to the need for liberation and provision in the here and now. Having performed his labor (of interpretation), his request is that of one who expects to receive justice and proper payment or reward, in this case, the reward of freedom ("bring me out of this house"). True to Joseph's prophetic interpretation, the butler is restored to favor by Pharaoh, only to break his promise: "Yet did not the chief butler remember Joseph but forgot him" (Genesis 40:23). Like Joseph, Wilson's authorship is labor that demands remembrance and material reward (she is financially destitute and needs to sell her story for money). Writing out of economic bondage, Wilson tells a tale of northern indenture in which the multiple strains of Joseph's saga are bound together in the interlocking complicities of race, gender, and class. Yet she takes the Joseph story further by telling a story that extends the bondage and freedom narratives to a cultural critique of gender and color in nineteenth-century America.

Although the butler and the baker dream different dreams with opposite consequences (the butler is restored to favor, while the baker is executed), the biblical narrator's reporting of the dream event is strangely ambiguous: "And they dreamed a dream both of them, each man his dream in one night, each man *according to the interpretation of his dream*" (Genesis 40:5, emphasis added). This phrasing emphasizes simultaneously unity and multiplicity, sameness and difference. Moreover, the ambiguity caused by shifts between singular and plural pronouns reveals the social grounding of the dream via interpretation as social meaning. Each man dreams in relation to the power of the Pharaoh, who determines guilt or innocence, death or life. Joseph's interpretive ability, attributed to God as its source, resides, at least in part, in his understanding of the social text of power. Similarly in *Our Nig*, the bourgeois family and American race relations are "two dreams" that are "one," as patriarchal domestic relations and American slavery come together in the "Two-Story White House" of the novel's setting. Wilson is telling, literally and figuratively, two stories at once: Frado, as the "Joseph" within the narrative, interprets the power dynamic within the Bellmont household, while at the same time the narrator extrapolates the significance of Frado's interpretation for the "gentle reader" in light of Wilson's overall authorial purpose.

Similar to the Joseph text in the Bible, *Our Nig* begins with narratives of family betrayal. Frado's poor, white mother is first betrayed by a white lover who promises to elevate her station through marriage. Having "surrendered to him a priceless gem," her virtue, Mag is abandoned along with the unnamed lover's "other victims" (6). Mag then marries Frado's father Jim, a "kind-hearted African" (9), a liaison that, even with the legality of marriage, lowers her status even further in the eyes of white society. Upon Jim's death, Mag takes up with Seth, another black man, eschewing "the rite of civilization or Christianity" (16), descending even lower on the social scale. The novel begins, then, like the Genesis of the Bible with a narrative of loss and original fall from social grace that parallels the biblical insistence on original sin and loss of innocence.

At Seth's suggestion, Mag goes along with a scheme to "give [their two] children away" (16), perpetuating the cycle of abandonment and betrayal. That abandoning Frado to the home of the Bellmonts is tantamount to selling her into slavery is clear from the description of Mag and Seth, leading their children by the hand along the "weary march" (20), reminiscent of similar scenes of slaves being led to the auction block in novels like *Uncle Tom's Cabin* and slave narratives like *The History of Mary Prince a West Indian Slave*. It is, furthermore, Frado's entry into the American social symbolic, as white children taunt the interracial family from the schoolyard: "'Hallo!' screamed one, 'Black, white and yeller!' 'Black, white, and yeller,' echoed a dozen voices" (21). Narrated through a call-and-response structure, the children's cruel taunts suggest a societal consensus on the meaning of skin color. Although they are one family, Seth, Mag, and their offspring's claim to the title "family" is deconstructed at the very moment that the family is made to suffer very real fragmentation. They are, the American color-text says, no family at all, as each is assigned a different position along the hierarchy of race relations. It is also ironic that while Seth is described as African American, his name is Hebraic, which recalls the proslavery hermeneutic that reads Noah's curse of Canaan in Genesis 9 and the table of nations in Genesis 10 as scriptural authorizations for slavery (see chapter 2). Seth, as the "father" who is "not father," and who thus rejects fatherhood, is inscribed under the sign "black," conflating the figures of both Jim ("the kindhearted African") and Seth in a gesture of effaced paternity.

Significantly, Mag is unresponsive to the taunting. The narrator tells us that "she had passed into an insensibility no childish taunt could penetrate" (21). Mag's psychological paralysis, her "insensibility" to the societal figuration of race relations, leads to a reinforcement of her decision to break up her "family," as she "extend[s] the separation once so easily annihilated by steadfast integrity" (21). Thus the disintegration of the father-mother-child triad is linked to the fragmentation of the self (her "integrity"). To keep the family together by keeping her children would mean, for Mag, holding on to the evidence of her own acts of miscegenation. Earlier, Mag's alienation from the "sneering world" of white society (7) is represented by the cramped space of the "hovel" she inhabits after her first "fall," and to which she returns after Jim's death. However, in public venues like the schoolyard the American racial text enacts its power through repetition and dissemination. Yet as we might want to read Mag's "insensibility" as a liberating posture, a position that allows her to pass beyond the social text that would assign moral value to sexual contact between the races, the familial narrative reminds us that, in order to reject racial inscriptions that assign "norms" of sexual propriety, Mag must give up her mulatto children because they embody the painful nexus of sexuality and race. The children, then, become "texts" that would condemn her.

In the paragraph immediately following this racial and familial mapping, the (white) bourgeois family structure is portrayed through the chronotope of the Bellmont house, "a large, old-fashioned, two-story white house, environed by fruitful acres, and embellished by shrubbery and shade trees" (21).[7] Invoking the power of myth and sacred narrative within the framework of the sentimental, Wilson writes:

> Years ago a youthful couple consecrated it as home; and after many little feet had worn paths to favorite fruit trees and over its green hills, and mingled at last with brother man in the race which belongs neither to the swift or strong, the sire became grey-haired and decripid [sic], and went to his last repose. His aged consort soon followed him. The old homestead thus passed into the hands of a son, to whose wife Mag had applied the epithet "she-devil," as may be remembered. John, the son, had not in his family arrangements departed from the example of the father. The pastimes of his boyhood were ever freshly revived by witnessing the games of his own sons as they rallied about the same goal his youthful feet had won; as well as by the amusements of his daughters in their imitations of maternal duties. (21–22)

Clearly there are a number of deliberate biblical echoes here: among others, "the race which belongs neither to the swift nor strong" (Ecclesiastes, from the wisdom tradition) and the son that "had not departed from the example of his father" (Kings and Chronicles, from sacred history). More important for our purposes here, the passage inscribes the patriarchal home of the Bellmonts within a sentimental vision that recalls both the American cultural ideal of the family (in sharp contrast to the "family" of Seth, Mag, and Frado) and the narrative of Eden and the Fall in Genesis. Like Morrison's repetition of the Sally, Dick, and Jane story at the beginning of *The Bluest Eye*, this passage presents a vision of domesticity as mythic as it is socially "self-evident." In contrast to the family narrative of Mag, Seth (or Jim), and Frado that opens the novel, this vision of domesticity admits neither betrayal nor broken kinship bonds. Instead, through the figure of the two-story house, the narrator represents family bonding and generational continuity. The two-story house contains, here, two stories, overlapping narratives of two generations of Bellmonts, for whom the house signifies entitlement as sacred ("consecrated") space. The material means of economic status and wealth remain outside the frame because, presumably, the "youthful couple" inhabit this space as innocently as do Adam and Eve the Garden of Eden. The first Bellmonts become a kind of first man and woman of the family myth.

Significantly, this passage hints at what will become an ambivalent displacement of the patriarch/pharaoh in chapter three. We are introduced to the present Bellmonts obliquely through the family's patriarchal origins: "the old homestead passed into the hands of a son." The fact that "John, the son," is mentioned after the pronouncement of Mrs. Bellmont as a "she-devil" positions her as the serpent in the garden, reinscribing woman as tempter and threat to patriarchal ownership of sacred space (i.e., garden, house). Once named, however, "John, the son," is restored as reproducer of the family myth: he "had not departed from the example of his father." The momentary instability of a family named first through a woman as disrupter and tempter is forestalled through patriarchal continuity, as John's sons, we are told through the innocence of childhood games, were "about the same goal" as their father (22). Moreover, the marginal social position of women is emphasized, as "his daughters" (notice the possessive), perform "imitations of maternal duties" (22).

Like the taunting games of the disembodied children's voices calling out from the schoolyard, childhood "pastimes" mark the generational efficacy of gender relations. Yet once again we have the "closing" of a narrative whose reopening is foreshadowed. Informed that "John is wearing the badge of age" and that most of his children "were already seeking homes of their own," Aunt Abby makes an appearance as "a maiden sister" who "occupie[s] a portion of the house" (22). The house as chronotopic representation of generational patriarchy thus admits into its representational space a "barrenness" that disrupts the mythic promise of replication through reproduction and fecundity.

These gestures of disruption through antithetical characters—the "she-devil" Mrs. Bellmont and the maiden (and religious) Aunt Abby—gesture toward the real disrupter of the consecrated bourgeois family myth: the presence of Frado, whose presence is the entry point, the "imposition" (27), of the "black, white, and yeller" racial text into the white patriarchal home, which both shatters the family narrative and shows it to be, in fact, an illusion. Urging the family to "'keep her,'" Jack, one of the Bellmont sons, states that "she's real handsome and bright, and not very black either" (25), repeating, in condensed form, the color prejudice of the schoolchildren. Mary's announcement, "'I don't want a nigger 'round me,'" and Mrs. Bellmont's reply, "'I don't mind the nigger in the child,'" renames Frado even as she is repositioned within yet another configuration of "family" politics (25). In fact, the sense of ownership is complete when Jack responds to Mary's hesitation by saying, "'Poh! Miss Mary; . . . it wouldn't be two days before you would be telling the girls about *our* nig, *our* nig!'" (25–26). This repositioning away from family and into property status is complete when Frado is placed "in the L chamber" to sleep (26). To underscore Frado's "descent" in status, the narrator describes her as "in some relation to white people she was never favored with before" (28).

PARTUS SEQUITUR VENTREM: OF BLACK WOMEN BORN

Earlier I referred to *Our Nig* as a Genesis of the African American women's novel tradition. Somewhat surprisingly, the first character we meet in the novel is a white woman who is, we are told in the chapter title, "Mag Smith, My Mother." If, as I argue, Wilson's project is to construct a myth of origins for black female subjectivity, what are we to make of a black womanhood (in the form of Frado's traumatic "coming of age" story) that emerges out of a fallen white womanhood? How do we account for our entrance into a black woman's text through white (not black) maternity?

Claudia Tate, in *Domestic Allegories of Political Desire*, argues that Wilson tries to construct a "discourse of maternal desire" based on the construction of Mag as "an inherently good mother," and that Frado "does not hold her mother personally responsible" for her plight (35, 37). In this way Tate reads the novel as "a complex maternal discourse" that "provides Wilson with a double symbolic recovery of the lost mother" (both Mag Smith at the beginning of the novel, and Frado's own motherhood at the end).

I do not believe the question of whether Mag is a "good" or "bad" mother is at issue here, although the question of maternal culpability is germane to the discussion, as I will discuss below. Such debates conflate Frado, the narrator, and Wilson, assuming that Wilson herself was mulatto with a black father and white mother. It is true that the threshold of the Bellmont house marks a narrative and textual boundary signaled, in part, by the disappearance of first-person pronouns in the chapter headings after chapter three. But rather than speculate on Wilson's own parentage or her possible "loss of authorial control," I see this threshold as a sign of our entry into a different narrative mode—"life," as it were, giving way to "myth." That it is in the context of the Bellmont home that Frado is renamed "Nig" and repositioned as "slave" is significant, not because Wilson may have suddenly decided to fictionalize her autobiography, but because it indicates a progression in narrative strategy away from "intervention" in a "master narrative" to "appropriation and revision" of a prior story in order to foreground its delegitimation.[8] In other words, on a metalevel, Wilson goes from pointing to an "other" story via her interventions in the biblical Genesis narrative to voicing the "other" story by taking on the origin myth that truly shadows this text—the law of *partus sequitur ventrem*: "Children got by an Englishman upon a Negro woman shall be bond or free according to the condition of the mother."

This seventeenth-century Virginia law of crime and punishment proposes a crime that is not really a crime (the rape of black women by white men), which results in a punishment that is no punishment at all (the offspring of such encounters shall follow "the condition [slavery] of the mother"). In its sleight-of-hand, whereby black children are depaternalized and the rape of black women decriminalized, the law not only effaces paternity and sanctions (through economic incentive) the rape of enslaved black women by white enslavers, but it also constructs the condition of slavery itself as predicated on black female bodies. That is, the enslaved black mother becomes accountable for the chattel status of her offspring. The perniciousness of the statute, then, derives not only from its status as the law of the land but from its function as a peculiarly twisted myth of origins.

Researchers on slave law have commented that, given the patriarchal structure of English society at this time, the law of *partus sequitur ventrem* appears to have come "out of the blue." Yet, as I argued in chapter one, the law is an extension of patriarchy, since it reenacts a biblical understanding of women as the originators of sin and suffering, the original curse of female. Just as the biblical Eve, "the mother of all living," is represented as the originator of man's fallen, sinful state, here the black woman becomes the origin for the "fall" of millions of black children (male and female) into perpetual slavery, a feminization of the slave condition that (re)constructs black masculinity as well. Black people were enslaved, according to this legal myth-making, for one reason and one reason only: because they were of black women born.

It is this insidious myth that constitutes the "shadows" out of which emerge the first three chapters of *Our Nig*. Mag Smith, although racially white, is "blackened" by her "fallenness" (contaminated by intercourse with black men), even, paradoxically, as her whiteness remains stubbornly visible vis-à-vis the bodies of her mulatto children, particularly Frado. Contrary to readings of the novel that see the figure of Mag as evidence of Wilson's break with the "traditional" miscegenationist coupling of white male and black female, Mag's character remains tied to—and in fact stands in for—the black mother.

This "ethic of divine reversal" (Weems) echoes many disruptive displacements in the novel—from South to North, for example, and from Mr. Bellmont's patriarchal power to Mrs. Bellmont's womanly tyranny. Yet the figure of Mag as the white mother of black children is particularly disturbing. Patricia Williams's comments on the legal decision of Judge Sorkow in the Baby M custody case are very telling on the issue of "the not-so-subtle images of which mothers should be bearing which children":

> Is there not something unseemly, in our society, about the spectacle of a white woman mothering a black child? A white woman giving totally to a black child; a black child totally and demandingly dependent for everything, sustenance itself, from a white woman. The image of a white woman suckling a black child; the image of a black child sucking for its life from the bosom of a white woman. The

utter interdependence of such an image; the merging it implies; the giving up of boundary; the encompassing of other within itself; the unbounded generosity and interconnectedness of such an image. Such a picture says there is no difference; it places the hope of continuous generation, of immortality of the white self, in a little black face. (226–27)

That we are asked to imagine this scandalous image (contrasted, for example, with the unproblematic representation of the black Mammy with white children, even the black women who served as wetnurses for the master's children) is Wilson's way not only of interpreting the racial subtext of the American dream but of disrupting our "mortal vision."[9] Yet, whereas Williams's description seems to be of a disruptive countertext, Wilson's Mag Smith, in abandoning her children, particularly Frado, forecloses the potential counternarrative through a psychical *méconnaissance*. In the moment that Mag speaks the discourse of American Africanism in (mis)naming her own children—"'Who'll take the black devils?'" (16)—her whiteness becomes not an image of blurred racial boundaries proclaiming "there is no difference" (Williams) but rather a reinscription of racialized hierarchies.[10] This misrecognition is further reinforced in her rationalization of abandoning Frado due to the child's willfulness. To cite Williams's *Alchemy* again: "one of the things passed on from slavery, which continues in the oppression of people of color, is a belief structure rooted in a concept of black (or brown or red) antiwill, the antithetical embodiment of pure will" (219). Wilson's representation of a "fallen" poor white woman who is socially "black" yet racially white dismantles the conflation of blackness and servitude, race, and condition as they converge on the figure of the black slave mother. In this sense, she shows how the equation of blackness and enslavement is a discursive "marriage," a miscegenation of terms.

Ultimately, the law of *partus sequitur ventrem* is a shadowy misrepresentation of black women's sexual violation under slavery. In this way, the Tamar subtext, visible yet marginalized within the Joseph narrative, is affirmed as Wilson voices a story that remains to be told, as she admits in the preface to have "purposely omitted what would most provoke shame in our good anti-slavery friends at home." In this vein she exhorts the reader to "refuse not, because some part of her history is unknown, save by the Omniscient God. Enough has been unrolled to demand your sympathy and aid" (130). Through multiple displacements and disruptions, the text announces its own omissions, utters its own silences. Wilson is perhaps alerting us to the fact that the silences—the missing history—are precisely where the real story begins.

> The only way to achieve this suspension, to break the chain of crime and punishment/retribution, is to assume an utter readiness for self-erasure. And *love*, at its most elementary, is nothing but such a paradoxical gesture of breaking the chain of retribution.
>
> SLAVOJ ZIZEK, *Did Somebody Say Totalitarianism?*

> ... and the greatest of these is love.
>
> 1 CORINTHIANS 13:13 (NKJV)

CHAPTER SIX

and the greatest of these

EROS, PHILOS, AND *AGAPE* IN TWO CONTEMPORARY

BLACK WOMEN'S NOVELS

In *Canon and Creativity*, Robert Alter writes of the tension in modern writing between creativity as a modernist value and canon as a sign of scriptural authority:

> The engagement of modern writers with the Bible ... cuts sharply two ways. They frequently translate biblical motifs and themes into radically redefining new contexts.... At the same time, the Bible remains for them a value-laden, imaginatively energizing body of texts, helping make possible the novels and poems they write through the powers of expression and vision that inhere in it. (8)

Toni Morrison echoes this sentiment when she describes the Bible not as part of her reading but as "part of my life" (*Conversations* 97), and when she notes that her frequent choice of biblical names for her characters is "the gesture of getting something holy" (80).

At the opening of her 1993 Nobel Prize lecture, Toni Morrison relates a folktale about a blind seer, whom she reads as "the daughter of slaves, black, American" in an effort to comment on the nexus between language and power. That oppressive uses of language are efficacious to the point of *becoming* what they enact is central to Morrison's thinking:

> Oppressive language does more than represent violence; it is violence; does more than represent the limits of knowledge; it limits knowledge. Whether it is obscuring state language or the faux-language of mindless media; whether it is the proud but calcified language of the academy, or the commodity driven language of science; whether it is the malign language of law-without-ethics, or language designed for the estrangement of minorities, hiding its racist plunder in its literary cheek—it must be rejected, altered, exposed. (20)

Morrison's move beyond representation to embodiment also works, in her view, to reconceptualize the possibility of a nonoppressive, creative use of language. "Narrative," she writes, "is radical, creating us at the very moment it is being created" ("Nobel Lecture" 205–6). The power of (re)creation that resides in story can undo the damaging effects of oppression by meeting the language of those structures on its own terms. Moreover, the new liberationist story involves cooperation and interaction that repositions the roles of reader and writers as cocreators of the text. Thus the black woman as writer/prophetess encodes a hermeneutics of transformation within her literary text.

This chapter will situate the contemporary black women writers Sherley Anne Williams and Toni Morrison within the tradition of black women's biblicism from the nineteenth century through their extension of the Shulamite trope—"black but comely"—from the *Song of Songs*. Before returning to the *Song of Songs*, which I discussed in chapter one, I want to note that there are several words translated as "love" in the Hebrew Bible and New Testament. *Hesed* in Hebrew speaks primarily of the "unfailing love" of God, especially toward His covenant people, Israel (Metzger and Coogan 467–68). In the Greek New Testament, love is broken down into *eros* (human sexual love), *philos* (brotherly or communal love), and *agape* (divine or transcendent love). The interplay between these differing aspects of love is evidenced in Williams's and Morrison's novels. Unlike Zipha Elaw's and Hannah Crafts's earlier appropriations, which steer around the *Song of Songs*' erotics, it is within the sexual nature of the poem that Williams and Morrison locate black women's power and agency. Moreover, the black female erotic as sacred narrative is recovered within the framework of blessing (see pp. 16–18).

Ricouer's rubric of *Song of Solomon* interpretation as comprised of four epochs is a good starting place. Pushing beyond the four types of criticism—analogical transference, between typology and allegory, modern "allegorical" community, and abandoning allegorical interpretation—Ricoeur proposes a new term to signify a mediating level of interpretation. Thus his idea of "nuptial metaphor" mediates hermeneutically between the "sexual realism" of the literal (modern) readings and "matrimonial moralism" of allegorical (traditional) readings.

Ricoeur's use of "nuptial" as a way of representing the "obvious sense of the text," which allows "the nuptial as such" to represent "other configurations of love than that of erotic love" (274), resonates with Ann DuCille's concept of "coupling" in African American women's fiction:

> I use the term "coupling convention" both to destabilize the customary dyadic relation between love and marriage and to displace the heterosexual presumption underpinning the Anglo-American romantic tradition. I also use the term in

conjunction with African American literature to reflect the problematic nature of the institution of marriage for a people long denied the right to marry legally. Marriage is necessarily a historically complex and contradictory concept in African American history and literature. (14)

DuCille's use of the word "coupling," like Ricouer's "nuptial," thus deconstructs both the romance plot of wooing, courtship, marriage, and sexual consummation that modern allegorical readings of *Song of Songs* mandate (see LaCocque) and the Western feminist insistence on marriage as only an "oppressive, self-limiting institution" (14). Indeed, for nineteenth-century African Americans, she argues, "marriage rites were a long-denied basic human right—signs of liberation and entitlement to both democracy and desire" (14).

Significantly, *Song of Songs* begins with a woman's voice: "Let him kiss me with the kisses of his mouth: for thy love is better than wine" (1:2). The foregrounding of female desire is consistent throughout the erotic poem, including the female beloved's declaration in chapter seven: "I am my beloved's and his desire is toward me" (7:10). This is a stunning reversal of the curse on Eve in Genesis 3:16, where her desire is constructed unilaterally toward her husband.

While some readers of the poem have argued that the patriarchal inscription attributing the poem to Solomon—"The Song of Songs, which is Solomon's"—eclipses the female voice within male ownership of language, others have regarded the *Song* as emblematic of female erotic power. For example, Francis Landy writes: "The dominance and initiative of the Beloved are the poem's most astonishing characteristics. Metaphorically aligned with a feminine aspect of divinity, associated with celestial bodies, the land, and fertility, the Beloved reverses the predominantly patriarchal theology of the Bible. Male power is enthralled to her" (317). He adds, however, this caution: "the lovers live, however, in a patriarchal world" (317).

Andre LaCocque, however, argues that not only do we have a feminine voice within the poem but a female poet as well, noting that "it is not only possible but it is expected that a love song in the ancient Near East be written by a woman" (243). For LaCocque, "it is a woman's song from beginning to end and it puts the heroine center-stage" (243).

The Shulamite's opening declaration—"Look not at me because I am black, because the sun hath looked upon me"—raises the issue of the protagonist's outsider status—"my mother's children were angry with me; they made me the keeper of the vineyards" (1:6). Here, gender, race, and class are all operative as markers of difference, and all converge under the sign "blackness." The dark skin color is attributed at least partly to being exposed to the sun due to performing outside labor.[1]

The reference to "my own vineyard" resonates with other images in the poem, where the beloved is referred to as a garden (4:12–16) and her breasts described as "clusters of the vine" (7:8). At the poem's end, the beloved exclaims, "my vineyard, which is mine, is before me" (8:12), suggesting a progression to self-possession and the ownership of her sexuality. Thus I want to read the *Song* as a poem about desire, pleasure, and black women's ultimate possession of their bodies and selfhood through the reclaiming of their own sexuality, a right denied them by the institution of chattel slavery in the United States.

The most cogent reading for my purposes is Julia Kristeva in "A Holy Madness: She and He." Confessing that the *Song* is in many ways "a chest whose keys have been lost" (86), Kristeva points to the following major themes in the poem:

1. Love as the powerful antidote for death (8:6);
2. "Love as unacknowledged lament," with the lover and the beloved as "lovers who do not merge but are in love with the other's absence";
3. The assertion of woman: "it is she who speaks and sets herself up as equal, in her legal, named, unguilty love, to the other's sovereignty. The amorous Shulamite is the first woman to be sovereign before her loved one";
4. Freedom and agency of individuals expressed through consensual intimacy and pleasure: "the enunciation of the Song of Songs is very specifically individualized, assumed by autonomous free subjects who, as such, appear for the first time in the world's amatory literature." (86–89)

Andre LaCocque reads the *Song* as potentially even more subversive in its authorship, form, and content, arguing that "the poet allegedly uses an innocent language of courtship while at the same time defying customary institutions by presenting . . . a universe that is outright erotic" (236). Anchoring the poem's "subversive eroticism," for LaCocque, is not only a female protagonist who "does the talking" (241) but, in fact, the writer of the *Song*. LaCocque points out that "it is not only possible but it is expected that a love song in the ancient Near East be written by a woman" (243). Thus, *Song of Songs* conforms to generic practices of its culture of origin. As LaCocque summarizes: "it is a woman's song from beginning to end" (243).

Just as the probability of female authorship and the certainty of female voice have been muted within the interpretive history of the *Song*, allegorical and theological readings have domesticized its message: "to the *eros* of the poem was artificially opposed a disembodied *agape*" (LaCocque 251). The spiritualizing of the poem strips away even gender difference in an attempt to transcend the body altogether, as female and male lovers become translated as "asexual personae" (251).

"HE CHOSED ME": AGENCY AND DESIRE IN SHERLEY ANNE WILLIAMS'S *DESSA ROSE*

In Sherley Anne Williams's novel *Dessa Rose* (1987), a pregnant slave is sold south for her violent retaliation of her husband/lover Kaine's death. Dessa then escapes with other slaves from the coffle, only to be caught and imprisoned again, this time sentenced to death by hanging upon the birth of her baby. While in prison, she is interrogated by Adam Nehemiah, a white ethnographer with dreams of a bestseller, who attempts to extract her story for his own gain. With the help of a network of slaves, Dessa escapes again, ending up at the plantation of Miss Rufel, a southern white mistress who harbors runaways. After the birth of her baby, Dessa and other fugitives from Miss Rufel's plantation plan an elaborate escape to the west, in search of a space of unqualified freedom—in the tradition of the great American novel.

In an author's note, Williams lays out her artistic vision for the novel:

> Afro-Americans, having survived by word of mouth—and made of that process a high art—remain at the mercy of literature and writing; often these have betrayed us.... This novel, then, is fiction.... And what is here is as true as if I myself had lived it. Maybe it is only a metaphor, but I now own a summer in the 19th century. (ix–x)

Important for my reading here is Williams's insistence on an alternative representation of the "curse" of the dehumanization of slavery; "I now know," she writes, "that slavery eliminated neither heroism nor love; it provided occasions for their expressions" (x). Williams portrays the relationship between Kaine and Dessa—in which consensual intimacy and pleasure are represented as ultimate acts of resistance to a system that dehumanized African Americans through controlled sexuality—both in terms of violation of individual bodies and through the overall surveillance that marked all aspects of slave life. Moreover the novel traces Dessa's liberation from a series of misnamings, signified by the subtitles that frame each section of the novel: "Darky," "Wench," "Negress." These phrases are prevalent in the written discourse of the ethnographer, Adam Nehemiah, and constitute the curse on African American women's subjectivity that will be dismantled by Dessa's own storytelling at the novel's end.[2]

Her choice for this resistant sexuality is the biblical prototype of the *Song of Songs*. The opening prologue to *Dessa Rose* is almost a fictional account of the central theme of *Song of Songs*, pronounced at the poem's end: "love is as strong as death" (8:6), as Williams portrays the agency to choose one's love object, to be desired and desiring, as the very sign of freedom. In this sense, consensual heterosexuality[3] under slavery is represented as the "antidote," in Kristeva's language, to the death-dealing power of the slavocracy:

> He [Kaine] ran the tip of his tongue down the side of her neck. "Ain't no wine they got up to the House good as this—" fingers caught in her kinky hair, palms resting gently on her cheeks. "Ain't no way I'm ever going to let you get away from me, girl. Where else I going to find eyes like these?' He kissed her closed lids. "Or a nose?" He pecked playfully at the bridge, the tip. "Mouth." ... Talk as beautiful as his touch. (4)

In this passage, the erotic language transgresses the cramped space of the slave quarters where the scene takes place. More important, it resonates with several passages from the *Song of Songs* where the lovers describe one another's bodies in elaborate conceits:

> Let him kiss me with the kisses of his mouth: for thy love is better than wine. (1:2)

> Thou hast ravished my heart, my sister, my spouse; thou hast ravished my heart with one of thine eyes, with one chain of thy neck. How fair is thy love, my sister, my spouse! How much better is thy love than wine! (4:9–11)

A more striking example occurs in 4:2–5, rendered by Francis Landy in poetic lines:

> Thy teeth are like a flock of sheep that are even shorn,
>   Which came up from the washing,
> Whereof every one bear twins,
>   And none is barren among them.
>
> Thy lips are like a thread of scarlet,
>   And thy speech is comely;
> Thy temples are like a piece of pomegranate
>   Within thy locks.
>
> Thy neck is like the tower of David
>   Builded for an armoury,
> Whereon there hand a thousand bucklers,
>   All shields of mighty men.
>
> Thy two breasts
>   Are like two young roes
> That are twins,
>   Which feed among the lilies. (308)[4]

In *Song of Songs*, the Shulamite is depicted as equally desiring of her beloved and catalogs his attributes in 6:10–16. Similarly, Dessa insists on both Kaine's desire for her (a redirection of the circuit of desire under the Genesis "curse") and her own sexual desire and pleasure as signs of agency and autonomy. In the prologue, Carrie Mae, one of the slave women, opens up the subject of slave breeding, which forms the backdrop against which to view the relationship between Dessa and Kaine: "Massa done sent his butt down here to get it out of trouble: taking care that breeding business" (3). In this climate of regulated and controlled sexuality, Dessa emphasizes the importance of free choice. "He chosed me," she tells Nehemiah, "Massa ain't had nothin' to do wid it. It Kaine what pick me out and ask me for his woman. Massa say you lay wid this'n or that'n and that be the one you lay wid" (11).

Kaine (whose name, spelled with a K, signifies on the mark of Cain, referenced in the Hamitic theology) is both a gardener and musician, and it is his love-talk that marks Dessa's memory in ways that elude Nehemiah's attempts to "capture" her story in written discourse.[5] His loving words—blessings, if you will—are the catalyst to Dessa's determination for resistance and, ultimately, freedom. That Kaine's discourse comes in the form of a love song resonates strongly with the biblical prototype. One of Kaine's songs that Dessa recalls in captivity is itself a biblical intertext, alluding to the Noah story *before* the "curse of Ham" pericope:

> Lawd, give me wings like Noah's dove
> Lawd, give me wings like Noah's dove
> I'd fly cross these fields to the one I love
> Say, hello, darling; say how you be. (31)

The power of this rewriting, the image of taking flight just before the "fateful" pronouncement of Noah's curse, is not lost on Dessa. After singing this verse, she remarks, "Kaine just laught when Mamma Hattie say that playing with God, putting yourself on the same level His peoples is on" (32).

Dessa's allusion to the revisionary power of African American spirituals arises again during a session with Adam Nehemiah, whose name signifies both the Adamic "everyman" and the prophet Nehemiah, who is marked by his obsession with racial/ethnic purity in the Old Testament book that bears his name.[6] It is through Adam Nehemiah that Williams parodies the betrayals/cursings of written texts. In his journal entry of June 29, 1847, for example, Nehemiah has written: "As today is Sunday, I held no formal session with Odessa. But in order to further cultivate the rapport thus far achieved, I read and interpreted for her selected Bible verses." Later in that same entry, however, Nehemiah, whose whiteness rather than piety seems to qualify him to pray "briefly for the deliverance of [Dessa's] soul," mis-hears that biblical revision encoded in African American spirituals. Initially annoyed by what he calls Dessa's "humming," he asks her to sing the spiritual:

>   Gonna march away in the gold band
>   In the army by and by
>   Gonna march away in the gold band
>   In the army by and by
>   Sinner, what you going do that day?
>   Sinner, what you going do that day?
>   When the fires arolling behind you
>   In the army by and by?

Completely missing Dessa's reversal of the hierarchy of sinner and saint, which places Nehemiah and his ilk in the "flames," he comments, "It is, of course, only a quaint piece of doggerel which the darkies cunningly adapted from the scraps of Scripture they are taught." Taking the "scraps of Scripture"—even those historically sent to "curse" black and female subjectivities—and adapting them not only to suit their present condition but to open up a discursive space for reimagining the future is at the heart of black women's turning the curse to a blessing.

READING "THE SEXY PARTS OF THE BIBLE": MORRISON'S *SONG OF SONGS*

While Williams's use of the Shulamite trope works to dismantle the dominant discourse's restrictions of black women's sexuality and desire, Toni Morrison's novels push the boundaries of the trope into the realm of community. In Morrison's economy, *eros* (sexual love) and *agape* (divine, self-sacrificial love) are framed within the terrain of *philos* (brotherly, community love).

Few writers have made such lavish and complex use of the Bible as Morrison. From the names of her characters—Pilate, First Corinthians, Shaddrach, Ruth, Hagar—to the inscription at the beginning of *Beloved* from Hosea and Romans, Morrison's novels are laden with biblical tropes, phrasing, and intonations. As the title to Shirley A. Stave's edited volume suggests, the relationship of Morrison to the Bible is one of "contested intertextualities." As one writer has remarked: "those who know their Bible well will have special access" to Toni Morrison's canon (Pocock 281). Criticism about Morrison's biblicism has tended to focus on the relationship of her novels to the biblical Exodus or a loosely framed Christology.[7]

While the *Song of Songs* may seem like a "chest which has lost its key" (Kristeva), it may itself be an important key to unlocking the treasures of Morrison's artistic and intellectual vision. It is not my aim here to conduct an exhaustive survey of such a huge project; rather, I'd like to focus on the importance of the Shulamite trope in Morrison's oeuvre as it serves as a touchstone for so many of her novels. In "Through a Glass Darkly," Judy Pocock reads Morrison's 1977 novel *Song of Solomon* in light of its biblical predecessor, especially through Morrison's use of biblical names and typologies. I would like to extend Pocock's reading to suggest that the *Songs of Songs* is possibly the biblical urtext for much of Morrison's novelistic and discursive project, since elements of its poetics appear in several of her works. Not only does she exploit the subversive power of black female erotics in novels like *The Bluest Eye* (1970), *Sula* (1973), *Song of Solomon* (1977), *Tar Baby* (1981), and *Beloved* (1987), but she explores and "de-metaphorizes" (LaCocque 251) the allegorical interpretive tradition by insisting on the body as the site of narrative.

Just as the "curse" of *partus sequitur ventrem* is figured in *Dessa Rose* in the form of an imprisoned pregnant slave and carried through the tag lines of "Darky," "Wench," and "Negress," the prison-house of slave law comes up repeatedly in Morrison's novels in representations of what I call "lethal maternity." From Eva Peace's burning of her son Plum's drug-addicted body in *Sula*—"Is? My baby? Burning?" (48)—to Pecola's incestuously conceived and still-born baby in *The Bluest Eye*, the barrenness of Violet Trace in *Jazz*, the barren Ruby women in *Paradise*, and the (apparently) abandoning mother in *A Mercy*, Morrison consistently gives us a troubled maternity. The lethal-maternal figure, emblematic of black motherhood under slave law, references birth and death simultaneously as an iconographic reminder of a treacherous sexuality. The most chilling example of the contradictions of black maternity—the mother who simultaneously gives life and takes life away—is the character of Sethe in *Beloved*; no writer to date has surpassed Morrison's brilliance in rendering this disturbing tableau:

> Inside, two boys bled in the sawdust and dirt at the feet of a nigger woman holding a blood-soaked child to her chest with one hand and an infant by the heels in the other. She did not look at them; she simply swung the baby toward the wall planks, missed and tried to connect a second time, when out of nowhere—in the ticking time the men spent staring at what there was to stare at—the old nigger boy, still mewing, ran through the door behind them and snatched the baby from the arch of its mother's swing.
>
> Right off it was clear, to schoolteacher especially, that there was nothing to claim. (14)

This description, around which the entire novel has revolved, positions the reader in the consciousness of the slavecatchers (note the word "nigger" to describe Sethe and "old nigger boy" for Stamp Paid) and outside that consciousness, "staring at what there was to stare at." At the center of the horror of this representation is "a nigger woman holding a blood-soaked child to her chest"—a cruel take on nursing, especially given Sethe's history of having her milk stolen. Not only, Morrison suggests with this scene, did slave mothers struggle to nurture their children—a process interrupted by the economics of slavery—they, in fact, birthed "dead" offspring.

While I agree with Jean Wyatt that the mother figure in *Beloved* "occupies a contradictory discourse" (475), I disagree with her premise that "the novel's discourse . . . tends to resist substitution" (474). Instead, substitution, not in the sense of metaphor but allegory, is the primary drive behind the text. In the scene mentioned above, the substitution—blood for milk—is completed as the dead beloved is positioned as the substitutionary sacrifice for the living Denver in a curious evocation of the Christian eucharist.[8] That Sethe "reached for the baby without letting the dead one go" suggests an equivalence, as Baby Suggs "traded the living for the dead" (152). Moreover, Sethe's placing of the blood-spattered nipple into Denver's mouth causes Denver to take "her mother's milk right along with the blood of her sister" (152).

The undoing of the curse, represented by the lethal mother in Morrison's work, is often figured as a transitory or imaginary, but still very real, blessing. Two of Morrison's novels, *The Bluest Eye* and *Tar Baby*, address the issue of female desire and desirability that reenact the but/and contradiction of the Bible's *Song of Songs* 1:5. In her first novel, *The Bluest Eye*, Morrison relates the story of a little girl whose desire for blue eyes, the sign of normative white beauty standards, drives her to despair and insanity. In the afterword to the Plume edition of the novel (1994), Morrison reflects on Pecola's predicament:

> The assertion of racial beauty was not a reaction to the self-mocking, humorous critique of cultural/racial foibles common in all groups, but against the damaging internalization of assumptions of immutable inferiority originating in an outside gaze. I focused, therefore, on how something as grotesque as the demonization of an entire race could take root inside the most delicate member of society: a child; the most vulnerable member: a female. In trying to dramatize the devastation that even casual racial contempt can cause, I chose a unique situation, not a representative one. (210)

Based on a childhood memory of a very dark-skinned girl who wanted blue eyes, Morrison writes that "implicit in her desire was racial self-loathing" (210).

Similarly, in *Tar Baby* we are introduced to Jadine, the exotic "copper Venus," who is caught between cultures as an elite fashion model. Yet it is the image of the Woman in Yellow in the novel that represents a counterdiscourse of "transcendent beauty" (46) that proves devastating to Jadine:

> The vision itself was a woman much too tall. Under her long canary yellow dress Jadine knew there was too much hip, too much bust. The agency would laugh her out of the lobby, so why was she and everybody else in the store transfixed? The height? The skin like tar against the canary yellow dress? . . . She looked up then and they saw something so powerful it had burnt away the lashes. (45)

If Pecola's desire enacts the "but" in "I am black but comely," the woman in yellow is emblematic of the alternative translation: "I am black and beautiful." Her very presence is a direct refusal of the destructive version of racialized beauty and has the power to destabilize Jadine's entire sense of her self and world. That she is described as "unphotographable" (46) suggests that she breaks the field of vision that tropes blackness as unbeautiful.

In her provocative article, "Wounded Beauty," Anne Anlin Cheng writes of a fundamental *méconnaisance* "surrounding the discourse of beauty at the intersection "between race and gender" (191). She notes:

> At the conjunction of racial and gender discrimination stands the woman of color, for whom "beauty" presents a vexing problem both as judgment and solution. That is, between a feminist critique of feminine beauty and a racial denial of nonwhite beauty, where does this leave the woman of color? Can she or can she not be beautiful? (192)

For Cheng, desirability based on racialized notions of beauty at least since the Enlightenment are inherently problematic, and "efforts at racial reclamation through slogans such as 'Black Is Beautiful' seem to announce injury more than remedy" (193).

Malin LaVon Walther writes of Morrison's revision of beauty in her novels as an attempt to refract the patriarchal gaze that constructs and constricts white women's sexuality. In this sense, Morrison is highlighting black women's desire for a specific type of male gaze that is objectifying and demeaning.

Morrison's choice of the name Breedlove in *The Bluest Eye* is important in several ways. First, Breedlove was the birth name of Madame C. J. Walker, the first female African American millionaire, who made her fortune inventing hair straighteners and skin lighteners for blacks in the late nineteenth and early twentieth centuries. The irony of Walker's entrepreneurship, involving beauty items that fed on African Americans' acceptance of white beauty standards, is not lost on Morrison. Crucial to the Breedloves in *The Bluest Eye* is a debilitating self-hatred:

> they believed they were ugly. Although their poverty was traditional and stultifying, it was not unique. But their ugliness was unique. No one could have convinced them that they were not relentlessly and aggressively ugly. . . . Mrs.

Breedlove, Sammy Breedlove, and Pecola Breedlove—wore their ugliness, put it on, so to speak, although it did not belong to them. (38)

That ugliness is constructed and not natural is clear from this passage. The Breedloves' acceptance of an outward evaluation of themselves breeds, in fact, self-hatred that manifests itself in various ways in the novel, from Pecola's desire for blue eyes, to Pauline's preference for the little white daughter of her employer, to Cholly's rape of his own daughter.

There is, however, another sense in which Morrison employs the word *breedlove* as a signifier of the slave breeding culture mentioned in *Dessa Rose*, with its short-circuited desire. In sharp contrast is the desire for consensual sexual intimacy that drives both Pauline and Cholly Breedlove. Pauline's desire appears at the end of her first-person stream of consciousness narrative in the form of "musings, idle thoughts, full sometimes, of old dreaminess":

> His face is next to mine. The bed springs sounds like them crickets used to back home. He puts his fingers in mine, and we stretches our arms outwise like Jesus on the cross. I hold on tight.... I know he wants to come first. But I can't. Not until he does. Not until I feel him loving me. Just me. Sinking into me. Not until I know that my flesh is all that be on his mind. That he couldn't stop if he had to. That he would die rather than take his thing out of me. Of me. Not until he has let go of all he has, and give it to me. To me. To me. When he does, I feel a power. I be strong. I be pretty, I be young. (130)

The erotic equation of sexual desire with the power to *be* desired reenacts the erotic circuit of the *Song of Songs*. Rather than position women as objects of male desire, the woman here rewrites herself as subject of her own narrative. Yet Pauline cannot bring this narrative moment into the cultural symbolic of the novel, and it is this failure that opens the space for Cholly Breedlove's rape of his own daughter, Pecola. Indeed, the novel begins with the realization of the transgression of the incest taboo, the original "fall" that drives desire in the novel.

The pattern in Morrison, then, is the eruption of black women's erotic desire (black and beautiful) and the co-optation of that desire within the social structure of power (black but comely). Rebecca Degler, for example, reads Pecola as a figure of ritual sacrifice in *The Bluest Eye*, as the community "rids itself of ... what they deem as nasty or undesireable, in an effort to rid themselves of that undesirability" ("Ritual" 232).

Recalling Kristeva's themes from *Song of Songs*, other Morrison novels reverberate with different aspects of the poem. The theme that "love is as strong as death" figures in Morrison's 1977 novel *Song of Solomon*, as Milkman and

Guitar end in a deadly embrace, and in Morrison's *Beloved*, where Sethe's "too thick" love results in the death of her baby daughter.[9] Love as unacknowledged lament, where the lovers are "in love with each other's absence," could apply to Sula and Nel in *Sula*; it could also apply to Son and Jadine in *Tar Baby*, who, in the relatively isolated space of Eloe, read "the sexy parts of the Bible" to each other. *Beloved* is almost entirely about absence and lamentation as it dramatizes the pain of family separation that was a hallmark of American chattel slavery. Morrison's latest novel, *A Mercy* (2008), is possibly her deepest meditation to date on the human need to enact gestures of *agape*, even within the direst of circumstances. Moreover, these gestures cross all lines of gender, race, nation, and ethnicity in the novel.

appendix

TO "SAMPLING THE SCRIPTURES:

MARIA W. STEWART AND THE GENRE OF PRAYER"

SCRIPTURAL REFERENCES IN THE PRAYERS
OF MARIA W. STEWART

All citations taken from: *Productions of Mrs. Maria Stewart, Presented to the First African Baptist Church and Society, of the city of Boston*. Boston: Published by Friends of Freedom and Virtue, 1835. (Reprinted in Houchins, *Spiritual Narratives*.)

1. Prayer from *Religion and the Pure Principles of Morality* (10–11)

STEWART'S PRAYER	SCRIPTURE SAMPLED	TEXT / GENRE / CONTEXT
O, Lord God,	Genesis 2:4–3:24	First use of this address for God—Yahwist account of creation.
the watchmen of Zion	Isaiah 52:8, 62:6; Jeremiah 6:17, 31:6	OT Prophets
have cried peace, peace, when there was no peace;	Jeremiah 6:14, 8:12	OT Prophets
they have been, as it were, blind leaders of the blind.	Matthew 15:14	NT Gospels—words of Jesus (context: hypocrisy of the Pharisees)
Wherefore hast thou so long withheld from us the divine influences of the Holy Spirit?		
Wherefore hast thou hardened our hearts and blinded our eyes?	Exodus 7:13, 14; 8:15, 19, 32; 9:7, 12, 34, 35; 14:8; and other references to God's hardening of Pharaoh's heart	OT Pentateuch
	Isaiah 6:9–10	"And he said, Go, and tell this people, Hear ye indeed, but understand not; and see ye indeed, but perceive not. Make the heart of this people fat, and make their ears heavy, and shut their eyes; lest they see with their eyes, and hear with their ears, and understand with their heart, and convert and be healed."—OT Prophets
	Matthew 13:13–17	NT Parables of Jesus
	2 Corinthians 4:4	"In whom the God of this world hath blinded the minds of them which believe not, lest the light of the glorious gospel of Christ, who is the image of God, should shine unto them."—NT Epistle
It is because we have honored thee with our lips, when our hearts were far from thee.	Isaiah 29:13	OT Prophets

STEWART'S PRAYER	SCRIPTURE SAMPLED	TEXT / GENRE / CONTEXT
	Matthew 15:8; Mark 7:6	NT Synoptic Gospels, words of Jesus
We have polluted thy Sabbaths,	Ezekiel 20:13, 16, 21, 24	OT Prophets
and even our most holy things	Ezra 42:13; echoes Exodus 26:33, 34; 29:37; 30:10; 29:36; and 40:10; 13 mentions in the Book of Leviticus: 2:3, 10; 6:17, 25, 29; 7:1, 6; 10:12, 17; 14:13; 21:22; 24:9; and 27:28	OT Prophets OT Pentateuch (references to the building of the tabernacle) OT Pentateuch / Torah
have been solemn mockery to thee.		
We have regarded iniquity in our hearts, therefore thou wilt not hear.	Psalm 66:18	"If I regard iniquity in my heart, the LORD will not hear me" — OT Poetry
Return again unto us, O Lord God, we beseech thee,	Psalm 80:14	"Return, we beseech thee, O God of hosts" — OT Poetry
and pardon this the iniquity of thy servants	Numbers 14:19	"Pardon, I beseech thee, the iniquity of this people" — OT Pentateuch
	Echoes Exodus 34:9	"And he said, if now I have found grace in thy sight, O LORD, let my LORD, I pray thee, go among us; for it is a stiffnecked people; and pardon our iniquity and our sin, and take us for thine inheritance." — OT Pentateuch
	Psalm 25:11	"For thy name's sake, O LORD, pardon mine iniquity; for it is great." — OT Poetry
Cause thy face to shine upon us, and we shall be saved	Psalm 80:3, 7, 19	"Turn us again, O God, and cause thy face to shine; and we shall be saved" — OT Poetry
	Echoes Numbers 6:24–26	"The LORD bless thee, and keep thee: The LORD make his face shine upon thee: The LORD lift up his countenance upon thee, and give thee peace." — OT Pentateuch

(continued on next page)

1. Prayer from *Religion and the Pure Principles of Morality* (continued)

STEWART'S PRAYER	SCRIPTURE SAMPLED	TEXT / GENRE / CONTEXT
	Psalm 67:1	"God be merciful unto us, and bless us; and cause his face to shine upon us." — OT Poetry
	Psalm 119:135	OT Poetry
	Daniel 9:17	OT Apocalyptic
O visit us with thy salvation.	Psalm 106:4	"Remember me, O LORD, with the favour that thou bearest unto thy people: O visit me with thy salvation." — OT Poetry
Raise up sons and daughters unto Abraham,	Matthew 3:9	"God is able, of these stones to raise up children unto Abraham" — NT Gospel, words of John the Baptist
and grant that there might come a mighty shaking of dry bones among us,	Ezekiel 37:1–14	OT Prophets
and a great in-gathering of souls.	Exodus 23:16; 34:22	OT Pentateuch — harvest feast days
Quicken thy professing children. Grant that thy young may be constrained to believe that there is a reality in religion, and a beauty in fear of the Lord. Have mercy on the benighted sons and daughters of Africa. Grant that we may soon become so distinguished for our moral and religious improvements, that the nations of the earth may take knowledge of us;		
and grant that our cries may come up before thy throne like holy incense	Exodus 31:8	OT — Pentateuch (altar of incense)
	Revelation 8:3–4	"And another angel came and stood at the altar, having a golden censer; and there was given unto him much incense,

110 APPENDIX

STEWART'S PRAYER	SCRIPTURE SAMPLED	TEXT / GENRE / CONTEXT
		that he should offer it with the prayers of the saints upon the golden altar which was before the throne. And the smoke of the incense, which came with the prayers of the saints, ascended up before God out of the angel's hand." —NT Apocalypse
Grant that every daughter of Africa may consecrate her sons to thee from birth.		
And do thou, Lord, bestow upon them wise and understanding hearts.	Proverbs and wisdom literature	
Clothe us with humility of soul	1 Peter 5:5	NT Epistle
and give us a becoming dignity of manners: may we imitate the character of the meek and lowly Jesus;		
and do thou grant that Ethiopia may soon stretch forth her hands unto thee.	Psalm 68:31	"Princes shall come out of Egypt; Ethiopia shall soon stretch out her hands unto God" — OT Poetry
And now, Lord, be pleased to grant that Satan's kingdom may be destroyed; that the kingdom of our Lord Jesus Christ may be built up;		
that all nations, and kindreds, and tongues, and peoples	Revelation 5:9; 7:9; 14:6	NT Apocalypse
might be brought to the knowledge of the truth,	1 Timothy 2:4	NT Epistle
as in Jesus,		
and we at last meet around thy throne, and join in celebrating thy praises.	Revelation 7:9–12, reprise	NT Apocalypse

2. Meditations: Prayer A (27)

STEWART'S PRAYER	SCRIPTURE SAMPLED	TEXT / GENRE / CONTEXT
O thou King eternal, immortal, invisible, and only wise God	1 Timothy 1:17	"Now unto the King eternal, immortal, invisible, the only wise God, be honor and glory for ever and ever. Amen." —NT Epistle
before whom angels bow and	Isaiah 6:2	"Above it stood the seraphims: each one had six wings; with twain he covered his face, and with twain he covered his feet, and with twain he did fly." —OT Prophets
cry, holy, holy, holy	Isaiah 6:3	"And one cried unto another, and said, Holy, holy, holy, is the LORD of hosts: the whole earth is full of his glory." —OT Prophets
	Revelation 4:8	NT Apocalypse
is the Lord God Almighty	Revelation 4:8	"And the four beasts had each of them six wings about him; and they were full of eyes within: and they rest not day and night, saying, Holy, holy, holy, Lord God Almighty, which was, and is, and is to come."
True and righteous are thy ways,	Psalm 19:9	"The fear of the LORD is clean, enduring forever: the judgments of the LORD are true and righteous altogether." —OT Poetry
	Revelation 17:7; 19:20	NT Apocalypse
thou King of saints.		
Help me, thy poor unworthy creature, humbly to prostrate myself before thee, and implore that mercy which my sins have forfeited		

STEWART'S PRAYER	SCRIPTURE SAMPLED	TEXT / GENRE / CONTEXT
O, God, I know that I am not worthy of a place at thy footstool;	Psalm 132:7	"We will go into his tabernacles: we will worship at his footstool."—OT Poetry
	Isaiah 66:1	"Thus saith the LORD, The heaven is my throne, and the earth is my footstool: where is the house that ye build unto me? and where is the place of my rest?"—OT Prophets
	Psalm 110:1 (cf. Mt. 22:44; Mk. 12:36; Lk 20:43; Acts 2:35; and Heb. 1:13; 10:13—NT refs. to Jesus)	"The LORD saith unto my Lord, Sit thou at my right hand, until I make thine enemies thy footstool."—OT Poetry
but to whom shall I go but unto thee? Thou alone hast the words of eternal life.	John 6:68	NT Gospel
Send me not away without a blessing, I beseech thee; but enable me to wrestle like Jacob, and to prevail like Israel.	Genesis 32:24–28	OT Pentateuch—patriarchal narrative, with revision
Be graciously pleased, O God, to pardon all that thou hast seen amiss in me this day, and enable me to live more to thine honor and glory for the time to come.		
Bless the church to which I belong,		
and grant that when thou makest up thy jewels,	Malachi 3:17	"And they shall be mine, saith the LORD of hosts, in that day when I make up my jewels; and I will spare them, as a man spareth his own son that serveth him."—OT Minor Prophets—voice of God
not one soul shall be found missing		
Bless him whom thou hast set over us as a watchman in Zion.	Isaiah 52:8; 62:6; Jeremiah 6:17; 31:6	OT Prophets (see Prayer from *Religion* above)

(continued on next page)

2. Meditations: *Prayer A* (continued)

STEWART'S PRAYER	SCRIPTURE SAMPLED	TEXT / GENRE / CONTEXT
Let not his soul be discouraged.		
May he not fail to declare the whole counsel of God,	Acts 20:27	"For I have not shunned to declare unto you all the counsel of God."—NT History—voice of Paul
Whether sinners will hear or forbear		
And now, Lord, what wait I for? My hope is in thee.	Psalm 39:7	"And now, Lord, what wait I for? my hope is in thee."—OT Poetry
Do more for me than I can possibly ask or think,	Ephesians 3:20	"Now unto him that is able to do exceeding abundantly above all that we ask or think, according to the power that worketh in us,"—NT Epistle
and finally receive me to thyself.		

3. Meditations: Prayer B (30–31)

STEWART'S PRAYER	SCRIPTURE SAMPLED	TEXT / GENRE / CONTEXT
Our Father, which art in heaven, hallowed be thy name. Thy kingdom come. Thy will be done.	Matthew 6:9–10	"After this manner therefore pray ye: Our Father which art in heaven, Hallowed be thy name. Thy kingdom come. Thy will be done in earth, as it is in heaven."—NT Gospels—words of Jesus ("Lord's Prayer")
Enable me to say from my heart, Thy will be done, O God.		
The heaven is thy throne and the earth is thy footstool;	Isaiah 66:1; Matthew 5:35; Acts 7:49	OT Prophets; NT Gospels; NT History
neither may any say unto thee, what doest thou	Job 9:12	"Behold, he taketh away, who can hinder him? who will say unto him, What doest thou?"—OT Wisdom Literature
	Daniel 4:35	OT Apocalypse
But thou art the high and lofty One that inhabiteth eternity, yet will thou condescend to look upon him that is of a humble, and broken, and a contrite heart	Isaiah 57:15	"For thus saith the high and lofty One that inhabiteth eternity, whose name is Holy; I dwell in the high and holy place, with him also that is of a contrite and humble spirit, to revive the spirit of the humble, and to revive the heart of the contrite ones."—OT Prophets
	Psalm 51:17	"The sacrifices of God are a broken spirit: a broken and a contrite heart, O God, thou wilt not despise."—OT Poetry
As such, enable me, O God to bow before thee at this time, under a deep sense of my guilt and unworthiness. It was my sins that caused thee to arise in thy wrath against me.		
Be pleased, O God, to blot them from thy book,	Exodus 32:32	"Yet now, if thou wilt forgive their sin—; and if not, blot me, I pray thee, out of thy book which thou hast written."—OT Pentateuch

(continued on next page)

3. Meditations: *Prayer B* (continued)

STEWART'S PRAYER	SCRIPTURE SAMPLED	TEXT / GENRE / CONTEXT
	Psalms 51:9	"Hide thy face from my sins, and blot out all mine iniquities."—OT Poetry
	Revelation 3:5	"He that overcometh, the same shall be clothed in white raiment; and I will not blot out his name out of the book of life, but I will confess his name before my Father, and before his angels." —NT Apocalypse—words of Jesus
and remember them no more for ever. Bless the church to which I belong.	Hebrews 8:12; 10:17	"For I will be merciful to their unrighteousness, and their sins and their iniquities will I remember no more"; "And their sins and iniquities will I remember no more." —NT Epistle
Thine arm is not shortened that it cannot save, neither is thine ear heavy that it cannot hear; but it is our sins that have separated thee from us.	Isaiah 59:1–2	OT Prophets
Purge us from all our dross;	Isaiah 1:25	OT Prophets, voice of God
hide thy face from our iniquities,	Psalm 51:9	OT Poetry
And speak peace to our troubled souls.	Psalm 85:8	"I will hear what God the LORD will speak: for he will speak peace unto his people, and to his saints; but let them not turn again to folly." —OT Poetry
	Zechariah 9:10	OT—Minor Prophets
Bless thy servant, our pastor; let not his soul be discouraged;		
but may an angel appear unto him, strengthening him.	Luke 22:43	NT Gospel—Jesus in Gethsemane

116 APPENDIX

STEWART'S PRAYER	SCRIPTURE SAMPLED	TEXT / GENRE / CONTEXT
Bless all the benighted sons and daughters of Africa, especially my unconverted friends.		
Send them not away from thy presence into that lake that burned with fire and brimstone,	Revelation 19:29; 20:10, 14, 15; 21:8	NT Apocalypse
but magnify the riches of thy grace	Ephesians 1:7; 2:7	"In whom we have redemption through his blood, the forgiveness of sins, according to the riches of his grace"; "That in the ages to come he might show the exceeding riches of his grace in his kindness toward us through Christ Jesus."—NT Epistle
in plucking their souls as brands from the burning;	Amos 4:11; Zechariah 3:2	OT—Minor Prophet (see Prayer F); OT—Minor Prophet (see Prayer F)
and though I may long sleep in death before thou wilt perform this work, ye grant that in the resurrection morn we may all wake in thy likeness and our souls be bound in the sure bundle of eternal life.		

4. Meditations: Prayer C (34–35)

STEWART'S PRAYER	SCRIPTURE SAMPLED	TEXT / GENRE / CONTEXT
O Lord God,		
Paul may plant and Apollos water, but thou alone givest the increase	1 Corinthians 3:6	NT Epistle
We are sensible that without thee we can do nothing.	John 15:5	NT Gospel—words of Jesus
Vain are all our efforts without thy blessing.		
But, O Lord God, thou hast the hearts of all thy creatures in hand; and thou canst turn them whithersoever thou wilt.	Proverbs 21:1	OT Wisdom Literature
Strip the hearts of this people from their idols, we humbly beseech thee.		
Take off their eyes from beholding vanity.	Psalm 119:37	"Turn away mine eyes from beholding vanity; and quicken thou me in thy way." —OT Poetry
Thou canst glorify thyself in making them the monuments of thy mercy; and thou canst glorify thyself in making them the monuments of thy wrath. Glorify thyself in making them the monuments of thy victorious grace.		
Open their eyes that they may see their feet stand upon slippery places, and that fiery billows roll beneath them.	Psalm 73:18	"Surely thou didst set them in slippery places: thou castedst them down into destruction." —OT Poetry
And, O Lord God, wilt thou in an especial manner have mercy on our unconverted brethren.		
Soften their proud and rebellious hearts, and be not angry with them forever.	Psalm 79:5; 85:5	"How long, LORD? wilt thou be angry for ever? shall thy jealousy burn like fire?" ; "Wilt thou be angry with us for ever? wilt thou draw out thine anger to all generations?"—OT Poetry

STEWART'S PRAYER	SCRIPTURE SAMPLED	TEXT / GENRE / CONTEXT
O, Jesus of Nazareth, hast thou not become poor, that they might become rich?	2 Corinthians 8:9	"For ye know the grace of our Lord Jesus Christ, that, though he was rich, yet for your sakes, he became poor, that ye through his poverty might be rich."—NT Epistle
Is not thy blood sufficient to atone?		
Wherefore, O Lord God, hast thou hardened their hearts, and blinded their eyes?	Exodus, Isaiah 6:9–10; Matthew 13:13–27; 2 Cor. 4:4	(see Prayer from *Religion* above)
Wherefore has thou so long withheld from them the divine influences of the Holy Spirit?		(see Prayer from *Religion* above)
Open their eyes that they may see that they are going down to hell, as fast as the wheels of time can carry them. O stop them in their mad career!		
Grant that a grievous cry might be heard among thy professing children, in behalf of perishing souls;		
and may it be like the cry of the Egyptians in the night that thou didst slay their first-born.	Exodus 12:29–30	"And it came to pass, that at midnight the LORD smote all the firstborn in the land of Egypt, from the firstborn of Pharaoh that sat on his throne unto the firstborn of the captive that was in the dungeon; and all the firstborn of cattle. And Pharaoh rose up in the night, he, and all his servants, and all the Egyptians; and there was a great cry in Egypt; for there was not a house where there was not one dead."—OT Pentateuch
And not only for ourselves do we pray, but for all nations, kindreds, tongues, and peoples.	Revelation 5:9; 7:9; 14:6	NT Apocalypse

(continued on next page)

4. Meditations: *Prayer C* (continued)

STEWART'S PRAYER	SCRIPTURE SAMPLED	TEXT / GENRE / CONTEXT
Grant that an innumerable host, which no man can number, may be gathered in from the four winds of heaven;	Revelation 7:1, 9	"And after these things I saw four angels standing on the four corners of the earth, holding the four winds of the earth, that the wind should not blow on the earth, nor on the sea, nor on any tree" ; "After this I beheld, and, lo, a great multitude, which no man could number, of all nations, and kindreds, and people, and tongues, stood before the throne, and before the Lamb, clothed with white robes, and palms in their hands;" —NT Apocalypse
	Matthew 24:31	"And he shall send his angels with a great sound of a trumpet, and they shall gather together his elect from the four winds, from one end of heaven to the other."—NT Gospel—words of Jesus
and when the last trumpet shall sound,	Matthew 24:31	NT Gospel—words of Jesus
grant that we may be caught up into the clouds of the air,	1 Thessalonians 4:16–17	NT Epistle
and our ear saluted with the joyful sound, "Well done, thou good and faithful servant; thou hast been faithful over a few things, I will make thee ruler over many things; enter thou into the joy of thy Lord."	Matthew 24:31	NT Gospel—words of Jesus

5. Meditations: Prayer D (36–37)

STEWART'S PRAYER	SCRIPTURE SAMPLED	TEXT / GENRE / CONTEXT
O, thou sin-forgiving God,		
they that are whole need not a physician, but they that are sick	Matthew 9:12; Mark 2:17; Luke 5:31	NT Synoptic Gospels—words of Jesus
Lord, I am sick, and full of diseases.		
If thou wilt, thou canst make me clean.	Matthew 8:2, 3; Mark 1:40–41; Luke 5:12–13	NT Synoptic Gospels—words of leper to Jesus
Though my sins have been as scarlet, thou canst make them as wool; and thou they be red like crimson, thou canst make them whiter than snow.	Isaiah 1:18	"Come now, and let us reason together, saith the LORD: though your sins be as scarlet, they shall be as white as snow; though they be red like crimson, they shall be as wool." —OT Prophets—words of God
	Psalm 51:7	"Purge me with hyssop, and I shall be clean: wash me, and I shall be whiter than snow." —OT Poetry
Were it not that there is a sufficiency in thy blood to atone for the vilest, the view of my past sins and transgressions would sink me in despair.		
Do thou loose their bonds, and let the oppressed go free.	Isaiah 58:6	OT Prophesies—words of God
Bless thy churches throughout the world.		
Clothe thy ministers with salvation, and cause the saints to shout for joy.	Psalm 132:16	"I will also clothe her priests with salvation: and her saints shall shout aloud for joy." —OT Poetry—words of God
Grant that the time may soon come, that all may know thee from the rising of the sun unto the going down thereof.	Psalm 50:1; 113:3	

(continued on next page)

5. Meditations: Prayer D (continued)

STEWART'S PRAYER	SCRIPTURE SAMPLED	TEXT / GENRE / CONTEXT
Fire our souls with a holy zeal for thy cause, and let us not rest at ease in Zion,	Amos 6:1	"Woe to them that are at ease in Zion, and trust in the mountain of Samaria, which are named chief of the nations, to whom the house of Israel came!"—OT Minor Prophets
whilst souls are perishing for the lack of knowledge.	Hosea 4:6	"My people are destroyed for lack of knowledge: because thou hast rejected knowledge, I will also reject thee, that thou shalt be no priest to me: seeing thou hast forgotten the law of thy God, I will also forget thy children." —OT Minor Prophets
Whilt thou increase her number of such, and such only as shall be saved.	Acts 2:47	NT History
Bless our pastor with a double portion of thy Spirit.	2 Kings 2:9	Elijah/Elisha—OT History
Encourage his heart, and strengthen him in the inward man,	Romans 7:22	"For I delight in the law of God after the inward man." —NT Epistle
	2 Corinthians 4:16	"For which cause we faint not; but though our outward man perish, yet the inward man is renewed day by day." —NT Epistle
	Ephesians 3:16	"That he would grant you, according to the riches of his glory, to be strengthened with might by his Spirit in the inner man."—NT Epistle
and may he see the work of the Lord prosper in his hands.		
And now; Lord, what wait I for?	Psalm 37:9	OT Poetry (see Prayer A above)
Dispel every gloomy fear that pervades my mind, and enable me to hope in thy mercy, and to thee will I ascribe praises everlasting.		

6. Meditations: Prayer E (Note: After Meditation X on death of her husband) (42–43)

STEWART'S PRAYER	SCRIPTURE SAMPLED	TEXT / GENRE / CONTEXT
O, Lord God,		
when I consider thy heavens, the work of thy fingers, the sun, moon and stars, what is man that thou art mindful of him, or the son of man, that thou shouldst visit him?	Psalm 8:3–4	
Thou didst at first create man after thine image, pure and upright; but man, by his disobedience, fell from that holy and happy state, and hath involved all his posterity in guilt and ruin.		
Thine awful sentence was just: "Dust thou art, and unto dust thou shall return."	Genesis 3:19	
Help me to realize that thou art a consuming fire	Deuteronomy 4:24, 9:23; Hebrews 12:29	OT Pentateuch; NT Epistle
to those that obey thee not, and that thou art arrayed in terrible majesty.	Job 37:22	"Fair weather cometh out of the north: with God is terrible majesty."—OT Wisdom Poetry—words of Elihu
Thou chargest thine angels with folly, and the heavens are not clean in thy sight; how much more filthy and abominable must be man, who drinketh in iniquity like water?	Job 15:15–16	"Behold, he putteth no trust in his saints; yea, the heavens are not clean in his sight. How much more abominable and filthy is man, which drinketh iniquity like water?—OT Wisdom Poetry—words of Eliphaz
Thou canst not look upon the least sin but with abhorrence, and thou wilt by no means clear the guilty.	Exodus 34:6–7	"And the LORD passed by before him, and proclaimed, The LORD, The LORD God, merciful and gracious, long suffering, and abundant in goodness and truth, keeping mercy for thousands, forgiving iniquity and transgression and sin, and that will by no means clear the guilty; visiting the iniquity of the fathers upon the children, unto the third and to the fourth generation."—OT Pentateuch—self-naming of God

(continued on next page)

6. Meditations: Prayer E (continued)

STEWART'S PRAYER	SCRIPTURE SAMPLED	TEXT / GENRE / CONTEXT
But though thy name alone is so terrible, yet Mercy stands pleading at thy bar, saying, Father, I have died: behold my hands and my side!	John 20:27	"Then saith he to Thomas, Reach hither thy finger, and behold my hands; and reach hither thy hand, and thrust it into my side: and be not faithless, but believing."—NT Gospel—words of Jesus to "Doubting Thomas"
Spare them a little longer, and have mercy upon the souls that thou hast made.		
O God, help me to realize that "man that is born of a woman is of few days, and full of trouble: he cometh forth as a flower, and is cut down; yea, man giveth up the ghost, and where is he?"	Job 14:1	OT—Wisdom Poetry
And help me to realize that it is with great tribulation that we enter through the gates into the holy city.	Acts 14:22	"Confirming the souls of the disciples, and exhorting them to continue in the faith, and that we must through much tribulation enter into the kingdom of God."—NT History
Once more I beseech thee to hear the cry of thy children in behalf of the unconverted.		
O God, this great work is thine; thou alone canst perform it.		
My church and pastor I recommend to thee; it is all that I can do; and that thou wouldst supply them with all needful blessings is the prayer of thine unworthy handmaiden.	Philippians 4:19	"But my God shall supply all your needs according to his riches in glory by Christ Jesus."—NT Epistle

7. Meditations: Prayer F (45–47)

STEWART'S PRAYER	SCRIPTURE SAMPLED	TEXT / GENRE / CONTEXT
Almighty God,		
It is the glorious hope of a blessed immortality beyond the grave, that supports thy children through this vale of tears. Forever blessed be thy name, that thou hast implanted this hope in my bosom.		
If thou hast indeed plucked my soul as a brand from the burning, it is not because thou hast seen any worth in me; but it is because of thy distinguishing mercy, for mercy is thy darling attribute, and thou delightest in mercy,	Amos 4:11; Zechariah 3:2	OT Minor Prophets (see Prayer B above)
and art not willing that any should perish,	2 Peter 3:9	"The Lord is not slack concerning his promise, as some men count slackness; but is long-suffering to us-ward, not willing that any should perish, but that all should come to repentance."—NT Epistle
but that all should come to the knowledge of truth	1 Timothy 2:4	"Who will have all men to be saved, and to come unto the knowledge of the truth." —NT Epistle
as it is in Jesus.		
Clothe my soul with humility as a garment.	1 Peter 5:5	"Likewise, ye younger, submit yourselves unto the elder. Yea, all of you be subject one to another, and be clothed with humility: for God resisteth the proud, and giveth grace to the humble."—NT Epistle
Grant that I may bring forth the fruits	Romans 7:4	"Wherefore, my brethren, ye also are become dead to the law by the body of Christ; that ye should be married to another, even to him who is raised from the dead, that we should bring forth fruit unto God."—NT Epistle—parable of marriage

(continued on next page)

7. Meditations: Prayer F (continued)

STEWART'S PRAYER	SCRIPTURE SAMPLED	TEXT / GENRE / CONTEXT
	Galatians 5:22–23	"But the fruit of the Spirit is love, joy, peace, longsuffering, gentleness, goodness, faith, meekness, temperance: against such there is no law." —NT Epistle
of a meek and quiet spirit.	1 Peter 3:4	"But let it be the hidden man of the heart, in that which is not corruptible, even the ornament of a meek and quiet spirit, which is in the sight of God of great price."—NT Epistle—submissive wife
Enable me to adorn the doctrines of God my Savior,	Titus 2:10	"Not purloining, but showing all good fidelity; that they may adorn the doctrine of God our Saviour in all things." —NT Epistle
by a well regulated life and conversation.	1 Peter 1:15, 18; 2:12; 3:1–2	"Likewise, ye wives, be in subjection to your own husbands; that, if any obey not the word, they also may without the word be won by the conversation of their wives; while they behold your chaste conversation coupled with fear."—NT Epistle
May I become holy, even as thou art holy, and pure, even as thou art pure.	Leviticus 11:45	"For I am the LORD that bringeth you up out of the land of Egypt, to be your God: ye shall therefore be holy, for I am holy."—OT Pentateuch/Torah
	1 Peter 1:15–16	"But as he which hath called you is holy, so be ye holy in all manner of conversation; because it is written, Be ye holy; for I am holy." —NT Epistle
Bless all my friends and benefactors: those who have given me a cup of cold water in thy name, the Lord reward them.	Matthew 10:42 (also Mark 9:41)	"And whosoever shall give to drink unto one of these little ones a cup of cold water only in the name of a disciple, verily I say unto you, he shall in no wise lose his reward."—NT Gospel—words of Jesus

STEWART'S PRAYER	SCRIPTURE SAMPLED	TEXT / GENRE / CONTEXT
Forgive all my enemies. May I love them that hate me, and pray for them that despitefully use and persecute me.	Matthew 5:44 (also Luke 6:27)	"But I say unto you, Love your enemies, bless them that curse you, do good to them that hate you, and pray for them which despitefully use you, and persecute you."—NT Gospel
Preserve me from slanderous tongues, O God,	Psalm 31:20; 55:9; 78:36; 140:3	OT Poetry
and let not my good be evil spoken of.	Romans 14:16	NT Epistle
Let not a repining thought enter my heart, nor a murmuring sigh heave from my bosom.		
But may I cheerfully bear with all the trials of life.		
Clothe me with the pure robes of Christ's righteousness	Job 29:14	"I put on righteousness, and it clothed me; my judgment was as a robe and a diadem."—OT Wisdom Poetry—words of Job
	Isaiah 61:10	"I will greatly rejoice in the LORD, my soul shall be joyful in my God; for he hath clothed me with the garments of salvation, he hath covered me with the robe of righteousness, as a bridegroom decketh himself with ornaments, and as a bride adorneth herself with jewels."—OT Prophets
	Revelation 19:8	"And to her was granted that she should be arrayed in fine linen, clean and white: for the fine linen is the righteousness of saints."—NT Apocalypse
that when he shall come in flaming fire to judge the world, I may appear before him with joy and not with grief; and not only for myself do I ask these blessings, but for all the sons and daughters of Adam,		

(continued on next page)

7. Meditations: Prayer F (continued)

STEWART'S PRAYER	SCRIPTURE SAMPLED	TEXT / GENRE / CONTEXT
as thou art no respecter of persons,	Deuteronomy 1:17; 16:19; 2 Chronicles 19:7; Proverbs 24:23; 28:21	
	Acts 10:34; Romans 2:10; Ephesians 6:9; Colossians 3:25; 1 Peter 1:17; James 2:1, 9	
and as all distinctions wither in the grave.		
Grant all prejudices and animosities may cease from among men.		
May we all realize [sic] that promotion cometh not from the East nor from the West, but that it is God that putteth up one and setteth down another.	Psalm 75:6–7	
May the rich be rich in faith and good works towards our Lord Jesus Christ,	1 Timothy 6:18	"That they do good, that they be rich in good works, ready to distribute, willing to communicate;"—NT Pastoral Epistles
and may the poor have an inheritance among the saints in light,	James 2:5	"Hearken, my beloved brethren, hath not God chosen the poor of this world rich in faith, and heirs of the kingdom which he hath promised to them that love him?"—NT Epistle
a crown incorruptible	1 Corinthians 9:25	"And every man that striveth for the mastery is temperate in all things. Now they do it to obtain a corruptible crown; but we an incorruptible." —NT Epistle
that fadeth not away	1 Peter 1:4	"To an inheritance incorruptible, and undefiled, and that fadeth not away, reserved in heaven for you."—NT Epistle
eternal in the heavens	2 Corinthians 5:1	"For we know that if our earthly house of this tabernacle were dissolved, we have a

STEWART'S PRAYER	SCRIPTURE SAMPLED	TEXT / GENRE / CONTEXT
		building of God, a house not made with hands, eternal in the heavens."—NT Epistle
And now what wait we for?	Psalm 37:9	OT Poetry (see Prayers A and D above)
Be pleased to grant that we may at last join with all the Israel of God,	Galatians 6:16	"And as many as walk according to this rule, peace be on them, and mercy, and upon the Israel of God."—NT Epistle
in celebrating thy praises.		

8. Meditations: Prayer G (48–49)

STEWART'S PRAYER	SCRIPTURE SAMPLED	TEXT / GENRE / CONTEXT
O Lord God,		
As the heavens are high above the earth, so are thy ways above our ways, and thy thoughts above our thoughts.	Isaiah 55:8–9	"For my thoughts are not your thoughts, neither are your ways my ways, saith the LORD. For as the heavens are higher than the earth, so are my ways higher than your ways, and my thoughts than your thoughts." —OT Prophets—words of God
For wise and holy purposes best known to thyself, thou hast seen fit to deprive me of all earthly relatives;		
but when my father and mother forsook me, then thou dist take me up.	Psalm 27:10	OT Poetry
I desire to thank thee, that I am this day a living witness to testify that thou art a God, that will ever vindicate the cause of the poor and needy, and that thou hast always proved thyself to be a friend and father to me. O, continue thy lovingkindness even unto the end; and when health and strength begin to decay, and I, as it were, draw nigh unto the grave, O then afford me thy heart-cheering presence, and enable me to rely entirely upon thee.		
Never leave me nor forsake me,	1 Kings 8:57; Psalm 27:9; Hebrews 13:5	OT History; OT Poetry; NT Epistle
But have mercy for thy great name's sake. And not for myself alone do I ask these blessings, but for all the poor and needy,		
all widows and fatherless children, and for the stranger in distress;	Deuteronomy 24:17	"Thou shalt not pervert the judgment of the stranger, nor of the fatherless; nor take a widow's raiment to pledge." —OT Pentateuch/Torah

STEWART'S PRAYER	SCRIPTURE SAMPLED	TEXT / GENRE / CONTEXT
	Psalm 68:5	"A father of the fatherless, and a judge of the widows, is God in his holy habitation." —OT Poetry
	James 1:27	"Pure religion and undefiled before God and the Father is this, To visit the fatherless and widows in their affliction, and to keep himself unspotted from the world." —NT Epistle
and may they call upon thee in such a manner as to be convinced that thou art a prayer-hearing and prayer-answering God		
and thine shall be the praise, forever. Amen.		

notes

INTRODUCTION. The Bible and African American Women Writers: A Literary Witness

1. What I refer to as "the Bible in English" is the Protestant canon consisting of the Old Testament and the New Testament. The Protestant canon consists of sixty-six books—thirty-nine in the Old Testament and twenty-seven in the New Testament—and omits the Apocryphal books that form a part of the Roman Catholic scriptures. I am aware of competing canons, such as the Hebrew Bible or Tanakh; yet it is undoubtedly the Protestant canon, especially the 1611 Authorized Version (commonly referred to as the King James Version), that has had the largest impact on African Americans from the period of slavery to the present. When other translations are used, they will be specified in the text.

2. Several recent works establish African American women's literature as intellectual and theological work in its own right. These include Joycelyn Moody's *Sentimental Confessions* and Gay Gibson Cima's *Early American Women Critics*.

3. See Alter and Kermode, *The Literary Guide to the Bible*; Robert Alter's *Art of Biblical Poetry*, *Art of Biblical Narrative*, *World of Biblical Literature*, and *Canon and Creativity*; and LaCocque and Ricouer, *Thinking Biblically*. See also Shuger, *The Renaissance Bible*; Moody, *Sentimental Confessions*; Yolanda Pierce, "Hell Without Fires"; and May, *Evangelism and Resistance in the Black Atlantic*. On the invisibility of religion in English departments, see Jenny Franchot's important article, "Invisible Domain."

PART ONE. Troubling Hermeneutics

1. *Speculum humanae salvationis*, anonymous, 1450. For a complete text and commentary, see Adrian and Joyce Lancaster Wilson, *A Medieval Mirror*.

CHAPTER ONE. Talking Mules and Troubled Hermeneutics: Black Women's Biblical Self-Disclosures

1. See Michael Barre's excellent reading of this scene in "The Portrait of Balaam in Numbers 22–24." Barre not only offers insight into the story of Balaam and the donkey but places it within the wider scope of references to Balaam throughout the Hebrew Bible and New Testament.

2. Numbers 31:8; Jude v. 11. See also Deuteronomy 23:4–5; Joshua 13:22; 24:9–10; Micah 6:5; 2 Peter 2:15; and Revelation 2:14.

3. MacMahon, *Cause and Contrast*, 86; Tanner, *An Apology for African Methodism*, 52; Sancho, *Letters of the Late Ignatius Sancho*, 79; Holland, *Frederick Douglass The Colored Orator*, 64; and Harris, *Balaam and His Master*.

4. Lee appears to have been quoted (but not acknowledged) three years later in Lewis, *The Life, Labors, and Travels of Elder Charles Bowles*: "On the subject of woman preaching, Dr. Clark says, 'if an Ass could reprove the prophet Balaam, and a barnyard fowl could reprove Peter, may not a woman rebuke sin?' Although as Mrs. Child says, the classification of women with donkies and fowls, is not very *complimentary*" (30–31). Here the quote is attributed to "Mrs. Childs" (probably writer and abolitionist Lydia Maria Child). Since Lee's text appeared first, Lewis probably copied the passage from her. Earlier in the biography he writes, "During the winter of the third year, of his Jonah's life" (12), which echoes Lee's claim that "I was like Jonah" in her *Journal*. The possibility that Lee's texts may have influenced other writers calls for more study.

5. See Andrews, *Sisters of the Spirit*; Connor, *Conversions and Visions*; Moody, *Sentimental Confessions*; my own *Spiritual Interrogations*; Grammer, *Some Wild Visions*; Staley, *Holy Boldness*.

6. See *Dust Tracks on a Road*; Hurston reports on a folktale in *Mules and Men* called "The Talking Mule," which may be an oblique reference to the Balaam story.

7. See Jeffrey, *People of the Book*.

8. Isaiah 40:3.

9. A central concern in this book is that we resist automatically collapsing the spiritual into the social or psychological. Moody voices a similar concern in *Sentimental Confessions*: "To read African American holy women's writings without regard for their religious content is to misread them, even to distort them in search of significance—political, social, and cultural significance—that is actually ancillary to their theology and certainly inseparable from it" (20). It is my contention that when black women writers, whatever their theological orientation, venture into spiritual terrain, such a move is intentional and significant in its own right.

10. On the curse of Ham theory in Judaism and Islam, see also Yamauchi, *Africa and the Bible*, 22–27.

11. Hill, *The South and the North in American Religion*, 109.

12. Henry Louis Gates makes a similar connection between uses of biblical material to inflict both racism and anti-Semitism in "Sour Grapes: Ezekiel and the Literature of Social Justice."

13. Patterson, *Slavery and Social Death*.

14. Westerman, *Blessing in the Bible and the Life of the Church*, 18. All citations will be taken from the English translation. See Genesis 24:60, 27:29; Numbers 24:17–18; Deuteronomy 33:7; and Genesis 49:22–26.

15. Blessing in the New Testament is often associated with Jesus, who blessed children, meals, and the Last Supper or Eucharist.

16. Many translators attempt to divide the poem into sections based on speaker, making it read more like a play; but even this attempt at order is difficult due to several passages where it is difficult to assign gender to the line.

17. I will use the title *Song of Songs* or simply *Song* throughout this book to distinguish the biblical poem from Toni Morrison's novel titled *Song of Solomon*.

18. Ricoeur schematizes the movement in commentary as follows:

   1. Analogical Transference — encompassing the patristic age, which treats allegory as "amplified effects of reading" (277) as such readings are embedded in specific liturgical acts.
   2. Between Typology and Allegory — which he associates with Origen as the "founder of Western allegory."
   3. Modern "Allegorical" Community — views allegory as the true meaning intended by inspired author(s) of the text.
   4. Abandoning Allegorical Interpretation.

See Paul Ricoeur, "The Nuptial Metaphor," in LaCocque and Ricoeur, *Thinking Biblically*. I elaborate on Ricoeur's analysis in chapter six of this book.

CHAPTER TWO. Private Interpretations: The Bible Defense of Slavery and Nineteenth-Century Racial Hermeneutics

1. There are several editions of "Jefferson's Bible." I refer to the edition by Dickinson W. Adams, *Jefferson's Abstracts from the Gospels*. All subsequent quotations will be taken from this edition.

2. There is much debate whether "Deism" as a descriptive term accurately fits Jefferson's complicated and wavering religious allegiances. In his old age, Jefferson confessed, "I trust there is not a young man *now living* in the United States who will not die a Unitarian" (quoted in David Robinson, *The Unitarians and Universalists*, 23).

3. Kathi Kern provides an excellent analysis of the historical and cultural climate and reception of *The Woman's Bible* in *Mrs. Stanton's Bible*. Particularly helpful is her analysis of the racism and classism in Stanton's discourse (see chapter 3).

4. In referring to "writing" and "canon," Kort here echoes Derrida's designations of "writing" and "book" in *Of Grammatology*.

5. See Kittel and Friedrich, *Theological Dictionary of the New Testament*.

6. For example, Riggins J. Earl refers to proslavery exegesis as "intentional misinterpretation" (4–5), which does not account for the theoretical, cultural, or textual grounds from which such a category as "misreading" must be constituted. This type of elision is what I am critiquing here.

7. For example, in tracing the progression from biblical to natural authority, Kort locates the beginning of the concept of nature as a "Book" to be read in Old Testament Wisdom writings that urge readers to move from the Bible (text) to world (nature and society) as a way of living out in an activist sense their belief in God (becoming "doers of the word"). He traces the inversion of Calvin's idea that the saving knowledge of God prepares one to gain a renewed (hence truer) reading of nature to Bacon's view that

the reading of nature is preparatory to reading the Bible. Yet it is Locke's Deism that proved the pivotal location for the decentering of biblical authority and the authorizing of nature. For Kort, Locke's belief that "knowledge received from reading nature can be trusted absolutely" (45) betrays as much a faith in the certainty of observable natural phenomenon as a distrust of language and textuality. Ultimately it is Thomas Paine, in Kort's account, who takes the next step to displant the Bible with nature (49). This "usurpation" of authority, to borrow Kort's terminology, is founded on Paine's (and Locke's, and possibly Jefferson's) quest for certainty, the quality that will now become the precondition for reading the Bible during the Enlightenment, which sets the tone for the rationalistic underpinnings of nineteenth-century American biblical hermeneutics.

8. See Frei, *Eclipse of Biblical Narrative* and "The 'Literal Reading' in Christian Tradition." See VanHoozer, *Is There a Meaning in This Text?* See Theophus Smith, *Conjuring Culture*, 256 n. 15.

9. For the difference between literal, literalistic, and allegorical, see VanHoozer, *Is There A Meaning in this Text?* and Frei, *The Eclipse of Biblical Narrative* and "The 'Literal Reading' In Christian Tradition."

10. Clarke, *Holy Bible Containing the Old Testament*, 130.

11. See Hood, *Begrimed and Black*, especially 155–81.

12. I am indebted for most of the information on the slave missions system to Janet Duitsman Cornelius's excellent study, *Slave Missions and the Black Church in the Antebellum South*.

13. See William L. Andrews's provocative article, "*The Confessions of Nat Turner*: Memoir of a Martyr or Testament of a Terrorist?"

14. See Gates, *The Classic Slave Narratives*.

15. See Leverenz, *Manhood and the American Renaissance*.

16. See Sterling Stuckey, "'My Burden Lifted': Frederick Douglass, the Bible, and Slave Culture," in Wimbush, *African Americans and the Bible*, 251–65. The debate with Garnet is also discussed in Callahan, *The Talking Book*, 21–25.

17. On the establishment and activities of the American Bible Society, see Gutjahr, *An American Bible*.

18. By contrast, this period also saw many elaborately illustrated editions of the Bible by printers such as Matthew Carey and Isaiah Thomas, some weighing as much as thirteen pounds. See Gutjahr, *An American Bible*.

19. See Bassard, *Spiritual Interrogations*.

20. H. Shelton Smith sees racism as a transgression against the *imago dei*, the pronouncement that humanity is fashioned in the image of God. See *In His Image*, especially chapter one.

21. See Anthony Thiselton's discussion of Frei's work in Lundin, Thiselton, and Walhout, *The Promise of Hermeneutics*, 162–63. See also Frei's *Eclipse of Biblical Narrative*.

22. The first of the two Simon poems features the African Simon of Cyrene, who carried the Cross after Jesus stumbled on the way to Gogotha, a scene related in all three of the synoptic gospels (Matthew 27:32; Mark 15:21; and Luke 23:26). The second is set at the

home of Simon the leper, another outcast figure in the gospels (Matthew 26:6–13; Mark 14:3; John 11:1–2 and 12:3), but features the prostitute Mary, who scandalously anoints Jesus's feet and wipes them with her hair.

23. See Boyd, *Discarded Legacy*; Peterson, *"Doers of the Word"*; Foster, *A Brighter Coming Day* and *Written By Herself*; and Graham, Introduction, *Complete Poems of Frances E. W. Harper*.

24. Melba Joyce Boyd remarks that this poem shares a title with a published anti- and pro-slavery debate in Louisville, Kentucky, in 1851. While the title may be coincidental, Harper would definitely have been exposed to debates like the 1845 debate between Rice and Blanchard, discussed above. The midwestern and border states, both North and South, seem to have served often as venues for such contests.

25. Melba Joyce Boyd assumes the poem "The Bible Defense of Slavery" is taken from a published debate by the same title that took place in Louisville, Kentucky, in 1851. These volumes of published debates were quite common, especially in the Midwest and border states. Harper could have based the poem on any such event, not necessarily the one from Kentucky.

26. See Blanchard, *A Debate on Slavery*.

27. Here I agree with Cain Hope Felder, *Troubling Biblical Waters*, in taking seriously African American understandings of the Bible as proceeding from a New Testament perspective. On the Exodus typology, see Theophus Smith's *Conjuring Culture*. Harper's longest poem, *Moses: A Story of the Nile*, has been treated extensively by Melba Joyce Boyd in *Discarded Legacy*. For this analysis, I will focus on the other biblical poems in Harper's canon.

28. William Sumner Jenkins notes that slaveholders relied on Genesis 9:20–27, Leviticus 25:44–46, and Philemon as the main texts in their arguments.

29. See Blanchard, *A Debate on Slavery*, and Barnes, *An Inquiry into the Scriptural Views of Slavery*. Blanchard cites Rice's proslavery argument that "Christ and his apostles did not denounce slave-holding, in so many words, or forbid it" as evidence that Jesus approved of slavery (427). Barnes refutes this same view, noting "nothing then can be inferred from the silence of the Savior on the subject" (244). Blanchard's point that "the Bible also denounces slavery, whenever it denounces oppression" is well taken (429), and it is echoed in Barnes's statement that "there is almost nothing which is more frequently adverted to in the Bible, than oppression" (358). Barnes also points out that Jesus himself, as a Jew under Roman rule, was an oppressed person.

30. Melba Joyce Boyd claims that the poem, along with Harper's other religious poems, represents a "more modern interpretation" of the Bible account (71–72). Carla Peterson reads the poem in light of the "sentimental discourse" (127) of nineteenth-century women's literature. Yet neither Boyd nor Peterson analyzes closely the Bible passage from which the poem is drawn in their brief readings. Both women assume the pericope is from Mark 7:24–30, but on closer inspection, Harper is probably relying on a composite portrait from both Mark and Matthew, drawing most heavily on the account in Matthew 15:21–28.

31. See Yellin, *Women and Sisters*.

CHAPTER THREE. Sampling the Scriptures: Maria W. Stewart and the Genre of Prayer

1. See Richardson, *Maria W. Stewart, America's First Black Woman Political Writer*; Peterson, "*Doers of the Word*"; Moody, *Sentimental Confessions*; and May, *Evangelism and Resistance in the Black Atlantic*. See also Stewart, *Productions of Mrs. Maria W. Stewart Spiritual Narratives*. The Oxford Edition, part of the Schomburg Library of Nineteenth-Century Black Women Writers, contains a facsimile reprint of the original 1835 edition of Stewart's *Productions of Mrs. Maria W. Stewart, Presented to the First African Baptist Church and Society, of the City of Boston* (Boston: Friends of Freedom and Virtue, 1835). All citations from Stewart's *Productions* will be taken from this edition.

2. Stewart was to publish yet another version of her writings in 1879 after finally successfully suing for her widow's pension. She used the money to fund the publications of *Meditations From the Pen of Mrs. Maria W. Stewart*, which in addition to the earlier writings included a short biographical sketch, bringing her life up to date.

3. The first black woman to publish a book of essays is Ann Plato of Hartford, Connecticut, in 1841. Stewart's early venture into this genre, however, places her within the overall American interest in this form by such figures as Ralph Waldo Emerson, Henry David Thoreau, Margaret Fuller, and others. It is interesting that the essay, or *belles letters*, form coincides with the decades often called "the golden age of American oratory," since the essay as a literary space often paralleled the space of the lecture platform.

4. See, for example, the slave narrative of Harriet Jacobs, *Incidents in the Life of a Slave Girl*, and Harriet E. Wilson's *Our Nig* for mentions of the rigors of domestic labor and the fact that such labor limited their time to write.

5. Compare Stewart's statement with this comment by Brother Lawrence, from a French monastery in 1666: "The time of business does not differ from the time of prayer, and in the noise and clatter of my kitchen, while several persons are at the same time calling for different things, I possess God in as great tranquility as if I were upon my knees" (*The Practice of the Presence of God* 8). On the connections between nineteenth-century black women spiritual writers and medieval mystics, see Houchins, introduction to *Spiritual Narratives*.

6. On gender exclusion in the African American church, see Jacqueline Grant and Evelyn Higginbotham. See also the spiritual narratives and testimonies of black women like Jarena Lee, Zilpha Elaw, Julia A. J. Foote, and Amanda Berry Smith. Black women's voices were reserved for singing, announcements, exhortation, and praying.

7. See Spencer, "Before the Feast of Shushan."

8. Stewart's prayers bear a striking resemblance to prayer movements within evangelical and charismatic churches in the United States in the 1980s, part of the current revival which cuts across race, class, denomination, etc. The practice known as "praying the scriptures" has been central to this current movement, as reflected in such volumes as *Prayers That Avail Much* popularized in Christian bookstores. These volumes are more like prayer primers and are topically arranged; therefore the prayers lack the movement and range of Stewart's. What they have in common with Stewart is the piecing together of scriptures from different parts of the biblical canon (cf. Book of Common Prayer and

other prayer books in Christian practice). While it is outside the scope of this chapter to go into more detail, it is interesting that Stewart's nineteenth-century practice should find a late twentieth-century counterpart.

9. The full title of the poem is *An Evening Thought, Salvation by Christ, with Penitential Cries: Composed by Jupiter Hammon, a Negro belonging to Mr. Lloyd, of Queen's Village, on Long Island, the 25th of December, 1760*. Another version of the poem is collected in Porter, *Early Negro Writing*, 529–31. The version in Porter is rendered as one long stanza, whereas Washington's version is collected as "Penitential Cries to God" and divided into quatrains, following the metrical pattern of couplets arranged in fourteenters. See *Conversations*, 3–5. See also O'Neil, *Jupiter Hammon and the Biblical Beginnings of African American Literature*.

10. *An Address to Miss Phillis Wheatley, Ethiopian Poetess, in Boston, who came from Africa at eight years of age, and soon became acquainted with the gospel of Jesus Christ*, dated "Hartford, August 4, 1778," and collected in Porter, *Early Negro Writing*, 533–37.

11. Twelve of the references are from the Psalms (Stanza 2, Ps. 135:2,3; Stanza 3, Ps. 1:1,2; Stanza 4, Ps. 103:1, 3, 4; Stanza 8, Ps. 34:6, 7, 8; Stanza 10, Ps. 84:1; Stanza 11, Ps. 34:1,2,3; Stanza 12, Ps. 71: 2,3; Stanza 13, Ps. 92:3; Stanza 14, Ps. 16:11; Stanza 15, Ps. 34; Stanza 18, Ps. 116; Stanza 21, Ps. 110:6). Four of the references are from the gospels (Stanza 9, Mt. 7:7,8; Stanza 16, John 4:13; Stanza 17, Mt. 6; and Stanza 19, Mt. 5:3). Three of the references are from New Testament epistles (Stanza 6, 2 Cor. 5:10; Stanza 7, Rom. 5:21; and Stanza 29, 1 Cor. 15:52, 53). Two stanzas reference Old Testament wisdom books (Stanza 1, Ecc. 12; and Stanza 3, Prov. 3:7). Stanza 3 has two references, one to the Psalms, one to Proverbs, and Stanza 5, as I noted earlier, is simply marked "Death."

12. Psalms 51:5. This is one of the penitential Psalms. Wheatley's prayer apparently went unanswered, as all four of the children she conceived died as infants, and she herself died in childbirth with the last one.

13. Washington includes footnote references for six direct quotations and one paraphrase. I have identified three more: Galatians 4:4 — "In the fullness of time," which invokes the Incarnation of Christ; Isaiah 9:1 — "the nations, which *now sit in darkness*"; and Psalms 68 — "*May Ethiopia soon stretch out her hands unto thee*," a verse also cited often by Stewart.

14. See also prayers by Daniel Coker (22–24), Rebecca Cox Jackson (39), Fannie Woods (41), Harriet Jacobs (45), and Sojourner Truth (55) for examples of prayers as narrative events rather than as free-standing texts; see Washington, *Conversations with God*. These prayers, as part of larger autographical writings, diaries, or journals, are also more experiential and contextual (within the framework of narrative) and show little or no concern with appropriating scriptural authority.

15. See Theophus Smith, *Conjuring Culture*. Note Wheatley's use of the phrase "our Modern Egyptians" in her letter to Samson Occom, February 11, 1774.

16. See Peterson, *"Doers of the Word,"* 66–67.

17. Other names for God that Stewart uses in her Meditations and prayers include: "Lord of hosts" (26), "O thou King eternal, immortal, invisible, and only wise God" (27), "Our Father" (30), "the Almighty" (33), "compassionate Redeemer" (36), "thou sin-forgiving God" (36), "Lord" (37), "Almighty God" (45), "Parent of mercies" (49), and "my Father" (50).

CHAPTER FOUR. Hannah's Craft: Biblical Passing in *The Bondwoman's Narrative*

1. Crafts, *The Bondwoman's Narrative*, ed. Henry Louis Gates Jr. All citations will be taken from this edition. Among those who doubt the authenticity of the narrative are Bloom, "Literary Blackface," and Adebayo Williams, "Of Human Bondage and Literary Triumphs." On "ethnic impersonator" autobiographies, see Browder, *Slippery Characters*.

2. See Goellnicht, "Passing as Autobiography."

3. See Elaw, *Memoirs*.

4. Here I disagree with Dickson D. Bruce, who argues that the only connection between the epigraphs and chapters is in "creat[ing] an interesting pattern evoking suffering and possibilities for deliverance" ("Mrs. Henry's 'Solemn Promise'" 140). The epigraphs weave a subtext that demonstrate Crafts's subtle argument about black women's biblical agency.

5. Paul Ricoeur, "The Nuptial Metaphor," in LaCocque and Ricoeur, *Thinking Biblically*, 265–303.

6. The phrase "the laws of the Medes and Persians" is common in nineteenth-century discourse as a figure for that which is fixed and unalterable, especially language. See, for example, Wiley, *Almanance* (1847); Simms, *The Wigwam and the Cabin* (1845) and *The Sword and the Distaff* (1852); Purviance, *The Biography of Elder David Purviance* (1848); Lewis, *The Life, Labors and Travels of Elder Charles Bowles* (1852). That all of these works appeared around the middle of the century accords with the estimated date of 1850 for Hannah Crafts's text.

7. Spencer, "Before the Feast of Shushan."

8. Interestingly, this pattern of biblical allusions does not solve the dilemma of Crafts's racial identity. The majority of writers referencing the Queen of Sheba are black, while those using the phrase "the Medes and the Persians" are predominantly white. I owe thanks to my research assistant, Alaina Hohnarth, for this discovery.

9. Compare with Morrison, *Paradise*.

CHAPTER FIVE. "Beyond Mortal Vision": Identification and Miscegenation in the Joseph Cycle and Harriet E. Wilson's *Our Nig*

1. Richards, "The 'Joseph Story' as Slave Narrative." Callahan, *The Talking Book*.

2. Lawrence Towner points out that Sewall's use of Ephesians is an intertextual reference to Paul Baynes's *An Entire Commentary Upon the whole Epistle of the Apostle Paul to the Ephesians* (London 1643), which reads chapter 5 on the relationship between masters and slaves as an injunction that "blackamoores . . . [be] perpetually put under the power of the master."

3. See Yamauchi, *Africa and the Bible*.

4. Theophus Smith provides an insightful reading of *The Selling of Joseph in Conjuring Culture* in his *Conjuring Culture*, 82 and following. See David Walker's *Appeal in Four Articles*, article I ("Our Wretchedness in Consequence of Slavery").

5. See Sandra Gilbert and Susan Gubar's classic, *The Madwoman in the Attic*.

6. For a study of proslavery sentiment in the antebellum north, see my "Crossing Over."

7. See Bakhtin, "Forms of Time and the Chronotope of the Novel."

8. I borrow the terms "intervention" and "appropriation and revision" from Mae G. Henderson's seminal essay on black women's discourse, "Speaking in Tongues," 35.

9. See Willis, *Picturing Us*.

10. See Morrison, *Playing in the Dark*; and Bay, *The White Image in the Black Mind*.

CHAPTER SIX. And the Greatest of These: *Eros*, *Philos*, and *Agape* in Two Contemporary Black Women's Novels

1. There is a long tradition in African American literature of light-skinned heroines being punished with outside labor in order to "darken" them, simultaneously rendering them less physically attractive and solidifying the conflation of race and class (slave) subjectivity. See Harriet E. Wilson's *Our Nig* (1859), William Wells Brown's *Clotel* (1853), Harriet Jacobs's slave narrative, *Incidents in the Life of a Slave Girl* (1861), and Hannah Crafts's *The Bondwoman's Narrative*.

2. On Dessa's utterance, see Mae G. Henderson's seminal essay, "Speaking in Tongues."

3. I use this phrase in the sense of Ann DuCille's term "coupling convention" to denote heterosexual unions that do not reinscribe heterosexism, but form part of the black resistance to dominant cultural notions of marriage. See Ann DuCille, *The Coupling Convention*.

4. See also *Song of Songs* 7:2–5.

5. Kaine's name is also an allusion to sugar cane, the cash-crop of the Caribbean. Dessa describes him as "the color of cane syrup" in the novel (58).

6. Adam Nehemiah is also a figure who signifies on the historical personage of Nehemiah Adams, author of the notorious *South-side View of Slavery*. See my "Crossing Over."

7. See the essays in Shirley A. Stave's *Toni Morrison and the Bible*.

8. I refer here, of course, to the Christian notion of drinking the blood of Christ as a sign of substituting Christ's death for the believer's life.

9. Similar ideas about love and the death of children appear in Gwendolyn Brooks's poem "The Mother" and Lucille Clifton's "the lost baby poem." I regard the representation of black motherhood and infanticide as a metaphor for the law of *partus sequitur ventrem*, as the mother is deemed responsible for the slave status (and consequent "social death," as Orlando Patterson writes) of her offspring. See chapter one of this book.

bibliography

Adams, Dickinson W., ed. *Jefferson's Extracts from the Gospels: "The Philosophy of Jesus" and "The Life and Morals of Jesus of Nazareth."* The Papers of Thomas Jefferson. Second Series. Princeton, N.J.: Princeton University Press, 1983.
Allen, Richard. "A Prayer for Hope." Washington 10.
Alter, Robert. *The Art of Biblical Narrative*. New York: Basic Books, 1981.
———. *The Art of Biblical Poetry*. New York: Basic Books, 1985.
———. *Canon and Creativity: Modern Writing and the Authority of Scripture*. New Haven: Yale University Press, 2000.
———. *The World of Biblical Literature*. New York: Basic Books, 1992.
Alter, Robert, and Frank Kermode, eds. *The Literary Guide to the Bible*. Cambridge, Mass.: Belknap Press, 1987.
Andrews, William L. "*The Confessions of Nat Turner*: Memoir of a Martyr or Testament of a Terrorist?" Wimbush, *Theorizing Scriptures*, 79–87.
———, ed. *Sisters of the Spirit: Three Black Women's Autobiographies of the Nineteenth Century*. Bloomington: Indiana University Press, 1986.
Bakhtin, Mikhail. "Forms of Time and of the Chronotope of the Novel." *The Dialogic Imagination*. Austin: University of Texas Press, 1982.
Barnes, Albert. *An Inquiry Into the Scriptural Views of Slavery*. Philadelphia: Parry and McMillan, 1855. Detroit: Negro History Press, 1969.
Barre, Michael. "The Portrait of Balaam in Numbers 22–24." *Interpretation* 51.3 (July 1997): 254–67.
Bassard, Katherine Clay. "Crossing Over: Free Space, Sacred Place and Intertextual Geographies in Peter Randolph's *Sketches of Slave Life*." *Religion and Literature* 35.2–3 (Summer–Autumn 2003): 113–41.
———. *Spiritual Interrogations: Culture, Gender, and Community in Early African American Women's Writing*. Princeton, N.J.: Princeton University Press, 1999.
Bay, Mia. *The White Image in the Black Mind: African-American Ideas about White People, 1830–1925*. New York: Oxford University Press, 2000.
Bibb, Henry. *Narrative of the Life and Adventures of Henry Bibb, An American Slave, Written by Himself*. New York: Published by the Author, 1849.

Blanchard, Jonathan. *A Debate on Slavery: Held in the City of Cincinnati, on the First, Second, Third and Sixth Days of October, 1845.* Cincinnati: W. H. Moore, 1846.

Bloom, John. "Literary Blackface." Gates and Robbins 431–39.

Boyd, Melba Joyce. *Discarded Legacy: Politics and Poetics In the Life of Frances E. W. Harper, 1825–1911.* Detroit: Wayne State Press, 1994.

Brother Lawrence. *The Practice of the Presence of God.* Old Tappan, N.J.: Revell, 1958.

Browder, Laura. *Slippery Characters: Ethnic Impersonators and American Identities.* Chapel Hill: University of North Carolina Press, 2000.

Brown, William Wells. *Clotel, or the President's Daughter.* London: Partridge and Oakey, 1853.

Bruce, Dickson D., Jr. "Mrs. Henry's 'Solemn Promise' in Historical Perspective." Gates and Robbins 129–44.

Buell, Lawrence. "Bondwoman Unbound: Hannah Craft's Art and Nineteenth-Century U.S. Literary Practice." Gates and Robbins 16–28.

———. *New England Literary Culture: From Revolution through Renaissance.* New York: Cambridge University Press, 1989.

Callahan, Allen Dwight. *The Talking Book: African Americans And the Bible.* New Haven, Conn.: Yale University Press, 2006.

Cheng, Anne. "Wounded Beauty: An Exploratory Essay on Race, Feminism, and the Aesthetic Question." *Tulsa Studies in Women's Literature* 19.2 (Autumn 2000): 191–217.

Cima, Gay Gibson. *Early American Women Critics: Performance, Religion, Race.* New York: Cambridge University Press, 2006.

Clarke, Adam. *Holy Bible Containing the Old Testament, the Text Carefully Printed from the Most Correct Copies of the Present Authorized Translation, with a Commentary and Critical Notes Designed as a Help to a Better Understanding of the Sacred Writings by Adam Clarke, Volume 1, Genesis to Deuteronomy 1811–1825.* New York: Ezra Sargeant, Printed by D. and G. Bruce, 1811–1825.

Coker, Daniel. "Prayers from a Pilgrim's Journal." Washington 22–24.

Cone, James. *God of the Oppressed.* New York: Seabury Press, 1975.

Connor, Kimberly Rae. *Conversions and Visions in the Writings of African-American Women.* Knoxville: University of Tennessee Press, 1995.

Copher, Charles B. "The Black Presence in the Old Testament." Felder, *Stony the Road We Trod*, 146–64.

Cornelius, Janet Dueitsman. *Slave Missions and the Black Church in the Antebellum South.* Columbia: University of South Carolina Press, 1999.

———. *When I Can Read My Title Clear: Literacy, Slavery, and Religion in the Antebellum South.* Columbia: University of South Carolina Press, 1991.

Crafts, Hannah. *The Bondwoman's Narrative.* Ed. Henry Louis Gates Jr. New York: Warner Books, 2003.

Degler, Rebecca. "Ritual and 'Other' Religions in *The Bluest Eye*." *Toni Morrison and the Bible: Contested Intertextualities.* Ed. Shirley A. Stave. New York: Peter Lang, 2006. 232–55.

Derrida, Jacques. *Of Grammatology*. Trans. Gayatri Chakravorty Spivak. Baltimore: Johns Hopkins University Press, 1976.

Deyle, Steven. *Carry Me Back: The Domestic Slave Trade in American Life*. New York: Oxford University Press, 2005.

Douglass, Frederick. *The Heroic Slave*. 1853. <http://docsouth.unc.edu/neh/douglass1853/douglass1853.html>

———. *Life and Times of Frederick Douglass*. New York: Collier Books, 1962.

———. *Narrative of the Life of Frederick Douglass, An American Slave, Written By Himself*. Gates, *The Classic Slave Narratives*, 243–331.

DuBois, W. E. B. *The Souls of Black Folk*. New York: W. W. Norton, 1999.

DuCille, Ann. *The Coupling Convention: Sex, Text, and Tradition in Black Women's Fiction*. New York: Oxford University Press, 1993.

Earl, Riggins J. *Dark Symbols, Obscure Signs: God, Self, and Community in the Slave Mind*. New York: Orbis Books, 1993.

Elaw, Zilpha. *Memoirs of the Life, Religious Experience, Ministerial Travels and Labours of Mrs. Zilpha Elaw, An American Female of Color*. Andrews, *Sisters of the Spirit*, 49–160.

Equiano, Olaudah. *The Interesting Narrative of Olaudah Equiano, or Gustavus Vassa, The African*. Gates, *The Classic Slave Narratives*, 1–182.

Fauset, Jessie Redmon. *Plum Bun: A Novel without a Moral*. Boston: Beacon Press, 1990.

Felder, Cain Hope, ed. *Stony the Road We Trod: African American Biblical Interpretation*. Minneapolis: Fortress Press, 1991.

———. *Troubling Biblical Waters: Race, Class, and Family*. Maryknoll, N.Y.: Orbis Books, 1989.

Fiorenza, Elizabeth Schussler, ed. *Searching the Scriptures: A Feminist Introduction*. Volume I. New York: Crossword Publishing, 1995.

Foster, Frances Smith, ed. *A Brighter Coming Day: A Frances Ellen Watkins Harper Reader*. New York: Feminist Press, 1990.

———. "Gender, Genre and Vulgar Secularism: The Case of Frances Ellen Watkins Harper and the AME Press." *Recovered Writers/Recovered Texts: Race, Class and Gender in Black Women's Literature*. Ed. Dolan Hubbard. Knoxville: University of Tennessee Press, 1997.

———. *Written By Herself: Literary Production by African American Women, 1746–1892*. Bloomington: Indiana University Press, 1993.

Franchot, Jenny. "Invisible Domain: Religion and American Literary Studies." *American Literature* 67 (1995): 833–42.

Frei, Hans. *The Eclipse of Biblical Narrative: A Study in Eighteenth and Nineteenth Century Hermeneutics*. New Haven, Conn.: Yale University Press, 1980.

———. "The 'Literal Reading' of Biblical Narrative in the Christian Tradition: Does It Stretch or Will It Break?" *Theology and Narrative: Selected Essays*. Ed. George Hunsinger and William C. Placher. New York: Oxford University Press, 1993.

Frye, Northrop. *Anatomy of Criticism*. Princeton, N.J.: Princeton University Press, 1971.

———. *The Great Code*. New York: Harcourt Brace Jovanovich, 2002.

Gates, Henry Louis, Jr., ed. *The Classic Slave Narratives*. New York: Mentor Books, 1987.
———. *The Signifying Monkey*. New York: Oxford University Press, 1988.
———. "Sour Grapes: Ezekiel and the Literature of Social Justice." *Seeing into the Life of Things: Essays on Literature and Religious Experience*. Ed. John L. Mahoney. New York: Fordham University Press, 1998. 271–76.
Gates, Henry Louis, Jr., and Hollis Robbins, eds. *In Search of Hannah Crafts: Critical Essays on The Bond Woman's Narrative*. New York: Basic Civitas Books, 2004.
Gilbert, Sandra, and Susan Gubar. *The Madwoman in the Attic: The Woman Writer and the Nineteenth-Century Literary Imagination*. New Haven, Conn.: Yale University Press, 1979.
Goellnicht, Donald C. "Passing as Autobiography: James Weldon Johnson's The Autobiography of an Ex-Coloured Man." *African American Review* 30.1 (Spring 1996): 17–33.
Graham, Maryemma, ed. *Complete Poems of Frances E. W. Harper*. New York: Oxford University Press, 1988.
Grammer, Elizabeth Elkin. *Some Wild Visions: Autobiographies by Female Itinerant Evangelists in 19th-Century America*. New York: Oxford University Press, 2003.
Grant, Jacqueline. *White Women's Christ and Black Women's Jesus: Feminist Christology and Womanist Response*. Atlanta: American Academy of Religion Academy Series, No. 64, January 1989.
Grimke, Archibald H. *Right on the Scaffold, or The Martyrs of 1822*. 1901. <http://docsouth.unc.edu/church/grimke/grimke.html>
Gutjahr, Paul. *An American Bible: A History of the Good Book in the United States, 1777–1880*. Stanford, Calif.: Stanford University Press, 1999.
Hammon, Jupiter. *An Address to Miss Phillis Wheatley, Ethiopian Poetess, in Boston, who came from Africa at eight years of age, and soon became acquainted with the gospel of Jesus Christ*. Porter, Early Negro Writing, 1760–1837, 533–37.
———. *An Evening Thought, Salvation by Christ, with Penitential Cries: Composed by Jupiter Hammon, a Negro belonging to Mr. Lloyd, of Queen's Village, on Long Island, the 25th of December, 1760*. Porter, Early Negro Writing, 1760–1837, 529–31.
Harris, Joel Chandler. *Balaam and His Master and Other Sketches and Stories*. 1891. Freeport, N.Y.: Books for Libraries Press, Short Story Index Reprint Series, 1969.
Hawley, John C., ed. *Through a Glass Darkly: Essays in the Religious Imagination*. New York: Fordham University Press, 1996.
Haynes, Lemuel. "A Prayer for New Birth." Washington 6.
Henderson, Mae G. "Speaking in Tongues: Dialogics, Dialectics, and the Black Women's Literary Tradition." *Changing our Own Words: Essays on Criticism, Theory, And Writing by Black Women*. Ed. Cheryl A. Wall. Piscataway, N.J.: Rutgers University Press, 1990. 16–37.
Higginbotham, Evelyn Brooks. *Righteous Discontent: The Women's Movement in the Black Baptist Church, 1880–1920*. Cambridge, Mass.: Harvard University Press, 1993.
Hill, Samuel S., Jr. *The South and the North in American Religion*. Athens: University of Georgia Press, 2007.

Holland, Frederic May. *Frederick Douglass The Colored Orator*. 1895. <http://docsouth.unc.edu/neh/holland/holland.html>

Hood, Robert. *Begrimed and Black: Christian Traditions on Blacks and Blackness*. Minneapolis: Fortress Press, 1994.

Houchins, Sue E., ed. *Spiritual Narratives*. New York: Oxford University Press, 1988.

Hoyt, Thomas, Jr. "Interpreting Biblical Scholarship for the Black Church Traditions." Felder, *Stony the Road We Trod*, 1–39.

Hurston, Zora Neale. *Dust Tracks on a Road: An Autobiography*. New York: Harper Perennial, 2006.

———. *Mules and Men*. New York: Harper Perennial, 1990.

———. *Their Eyes Were Watching God*. New York: Harper Perennial, 1990.

Jacobs, Harriet. *Incidents in the Life of a Slave Girl*. Gates, *The Classic Slave Narratives*, 333–515.

Jea, John. *The Life, History, and Unparalleled Suffering of John Jea, the African Preacher. Compiled and Written by Himself*. 1811. <http://docsouth.unc.edu/neh/jeajohn/jeajohn.html>

Jeffrey, David Lyle. *People of the Book: Christian Identity and Literary Culture*. Grand Rapids, Mich.: Eerdmans Academic Press, 1986.

Jenkins, William Sumpter. *Pro-Slavery Thought in the Old South*. Chapel Hill: University of North Carolina Press, 1935.

Jobling, David. "Ruth Finds a Home: Canon, Politics, Method." *The New Literary Theory and the Hebrew Bible*. Ed. J. Cheryl Exum and David J. A. Clines. Valley Forge, Penn.: Trinity Press International, 1993. 125–39.

Johnson, James Weldon. *God's Trombones: Seven Negro Sermons in Verse*. New York: Penguin Classics, 1990.

Johnson, Thomas L. (Thomas Lewis). *Twenty-Eight Years a Slave, or the Story of My Life in Three Continents*. 1909. <http://docsouth.unc.edu/neh/johnson1/johnson.html#john17>

Jones, Absalom. "Thanksgiving Prayer for the Abolition of the African Slave Trade." Washington 12–13.

Jordan, Winthrop. *White Over Black: American Attitudes Toward the Negro, 1550–1812*. Chapel Hill: University of North Carolina Press, 1995.

Kern, Kathi. *Mrs. Stanton's Bible*. Ithaca: Cornell University Press, 2001.

Kittel, Gerhard, and Gerhard Friedrich. *Theological Dictionary of the New Testament and Greek English Lexicon According to Semantic Domains*. Trans. Geoffrey W. Bromiley. Grand Rapids, Mich.: Eerdmans Academic Press, 1985.

Kort, Wesley A. *"Take, Read": Scripture, Textuality and Cultural Practice*. University Park: Pennsylvania State University Press, 1996.

Kristeva, Julia. "A Holy Madness: She and He." *Tales of Love*. Trans. Leon S. Roudiez. New York: Columbia University Press, 1987.

Lacan, Jaques. "The Agency of the Letter in the Unconscious." *Ecrits: A Selection*. Trans. Alan Sheridan. New York: W. W. Norton, 1977.

LaCocque, Andre, and Paul Ricoeur. *Thinking Biblically: Exegetical and Hermeneutical Studies*. Trans. David Pellauer. Chicago: University of Chicago Press, 1998.

Landy, Francis. "The Song of Songs." Alter and Kermode 305–19.

Lawrence, Joshua. *The American Telescope, by a Clodhopper, of North Carolina* 1825. <http://docsouth.unc.edu/nc/lawrence/lawrence.html>

Lee, Jarena. *Life and Religious Experience of Mrs. Jarena Lee, A Colored Lady*. Andrews, *Sisters of the Spirit*, 25–48.

———. "Prayer for Sanctification." Washington 14–15.

———. *Religious Experience and Journal of Mrs. Jarena Lee, Giving an Account of Her Call to Preach the Gospel*. 1849. Houchins, *Spiritual Narratives*.

Leverenz, David. *Manhood and the American Renaissance*. Ithaca: Cornell University Press, 1989.

Lewis, John W. *The Life, Labors, and Travels of Elder Charles Bowles, of the Free Will Baptist Denomination, by Eld. John W. Lewis. Together with an Essay on the Character and Condition of the African Race by the Same. Also, an Essay on the Fugitive Law of the U.S. Congress of 1850, by Rev. Arthur Dearing*. 1852. <http://docsouth.unc.edu/neh/lewisjw/lewisjw.html>

Lowery, Rev. Irving E. *Life on the Old Plantation in Ante-Bellum Days* OR *A Story Based on Facts*. 1911. <http://docsouth.unc.edu/neh/lowery/lowery.html>

Lundin, Roger, ed. *There Before Us: Religion, Literature, and Culture from Emerson to Wendell Berry*. Grand Rapids, Mich.: Eerdmans Academic Press, 2007.

Lundin, Roger, Anthony C. Thiselton, and Clarence Walhout. *The Promise of Hermeneutics*. Grand Rapids, Mich.: Eerdmans Academic Press, 1999.

MacMahon, T. W. *Cause and Contrast: an Essay on the American Crisis*. Richmond. Virginia, 1862. <http://docsouth.unc.edu/imls/cause/cause.html>

Marsden, George. "Everyone One's Own Interpreter? The Bible, Science, and Authority in Mid-Nineteenth-Century America." *The Bible in America: Essays in Cultural History*. Ed. Nathan Hatch and Mark A. Noll. New York: Oxford University Press, 1982.

Matter, E. Ann. *The Voice of My Beloved: The Song of Songs In Western Medieval Christianity*. Philadelphia: University of Pennsylvania Press, 1990.

May, Cedric. *Evangelism and Resistance in the Black Atlantic, 1760–1835*. Athens: University of Georgia Press, 2008.

McCaine, Alexander. *Slavery Defended from Scripture, Against the Attacks of the Abolitionists in the Methodist Protestant Church in Baltimore 1842. In His Image, but . . . Racism in Southern Religion, 1780–1910*. Ed. Hilrie Shelton Smith. Durham, N.C.: Duke University Press, 1972.

Metzger, Bruce M., and Michael D. Coogan, eds. *The Oxford Companion to the Bible*. New York: Oxford University Press, 1993.

Moody, Joycelyn. *Sentimental Confessions: Spiritual Narratives of Nineteenth-Century African American Women*. Athens: University of Georgia Press, 2003.

Morrison, Toni. *Beloved*. New York: Vintage Books, 2004.

———. *The Bluest Eye*. New York: Plume, 1994.

———. "The Nobel Lecture in Literature." *Toni Morrison: What Moves at the Margin: Selected Non-Fiction*. Ed. Carolyn D. Denard. Jackson: University Press of Mississippi, 2008. 198–207.

———. *Paradise*. New York, Plume, 1999.
———. *Playing in the Dark: Whiteness and the Literary Imagination*. New York: Vintage Books, 1993.
———. "Recitatif." *Norton Anthology of American Literature*. Ed. Wayne Franklin et al. 6th ed. 2007. Vol. E, 2252–66.
———. *Song of Solomon*. New York: Vintage Books, 2004.
———. *Tar Baby*. New York: Vintage Books, 2004.
Morrison-Reed, Mark. *Black Pioneers in a White Denomination*. Boston: Skinner House Books, 1994.
Nida, Eugene A., and Johannes P. Louw. *Greek-English Lexicon of the New Testament: Based on Semantic Domains*. New York: United Bible Studies, 1989.
Noll, Mark. *America's God: From Jonathan Edwards to Abraham Lincoln*. New York: Oxford University Press, 2002.
———. "The Image of the United States as a Biblical Nation, 1776–1865." *The Bible in America: Essays in Cultural History*. Ed. Nathan Hatch and Mark Noll. New York: Oxford University Press, 1982.
Northrop, Henry Davenport. *Treasures of the Bible*. Philadelphia: International Publishing Company, 1894.
O'Neil, Sondra A. *Jupiter Hammon and the Biblical Beginnings of African-American Literature*. Lanham, Md.: Scarecrow Press, 1993.
Patterson, Orlando. *Slavery and Social Death: A Comparative Study*. Cambridge, Mass.: Harvard University Press, 2007.
Payne, Alexander "Prayer for Dedication of a Church Edifice." *Washington* 36–37.
Peterson, Carla. *"Doers of the Word": African-American Women Speakers and Writers in the North (1830–1880)*. New Brunswick, N.J.: Rutgers University Press, 1995.
Pierce, Yolanda. *"Hell without Fires": Slavery, Christianity, and the Antebellum Spiritual Narrative*. Gainesville: University Press of Florida, 2005.
Pocock, Judy. "'Through a Glass Darkly': Typology in Toni Morrison's Song of Solomon." *Canadian Review of American Studies* 35.3 (2005): 281–98.
Porter, Dorothy, ed. *Early Negro Writing, 1760–1837*. Boston: Beacon Press, 1995.
Purviance, Levi. *The Biography of Elder David Purviance, with His Memoirs: Containing His Views on Baptism, the Divinity of Christ, and the Atonement. Written by Himself: with an Appendix; Giving Biographical Sketches of Elders John Hardy, Reuben Dooly, William Dye, Thos. Kyle, George Shidler, William Kinkade, Thomas Adams, Samuel Kyle, and Nathan Worley. Together with a Historical Sketch of the Great Kentucky Revival*. 1848. <http://docsouth.unc.edu/nc/purviance/purviance.html>
Raboteau, Albert J. *Slave Religion: The "Invisible Institution" in the Antebellum South*. New York: Oxford University Press, 1978.
Ramsey, Guthrie P. *Race Music: Black Cultures from Bebop to Hip-Hop*. Berkeley: University of California Press, 2004.
Richards, Phillip. "The 'Joseph Story' as Slave Narrative: On Genesis and Exodus as Prototypes for Early Black Anglophone Writing." Wimbush, *African Americans and the Bible*, 221–35.

Richardson, Marilyn, ed. *Maria W. Stewart: American's First Black Woman Political Writer: Essays and Speeches.* Bloomington: Indiana University Press, 1987.

Robinson, David. *The Unitarians and the Universalists.* Westport, Conn.: Greenwood Press, 1985.

Rohrbach, Augusta. "'A Silent Unobtrusive Way': Hannah Crafts and the Literary Marketplace." Gates and Robbins 3–15.

Saffin, John. "A Brief and Candid Answer to a Late Printed Sheet, Entitled The Selling of Joseph." 1705. Reprinted in Asner C. Goodell. "John Saffin and His Slave Adam." *Publication of the Colonial Society of Massachusetts* 1 (1895): 85–112.

Sancho, Ignatius. *Letters of the Late Ignatius Sancho, An African. In Two Volumes. To Which Are Prefixed, Memoirs of His Life.* Vol. 2. 1782. <http://docsouth.unc.edu/neh/sancho2/sancho2.html>

Sewall, Samuel. *A Brief and Candid Answer to a late Printed Sheet Entitled the Selling of Joseph.*

———. *The Selling of Joseph.* Boston: Bartholomew Green and John Allen, 1700.

Sherman, Joan R. *Invisible Poets: Afro-Americans of the Nineteenth Century.* Champaign: University of Illinois Press, 1989.

Shuger, Debora. *The Renaissance Bible.* Berkeley: University of California Press, 1994.

Simms, William Gilmore. *The Sword and the Distaff: Or, "Fair, Fat, and Forty." A Story of the South, at the Close of the Revolution by the Author of "The Partisan," "Mellichampe," "Katharine Walton," Etc. Etc.* 1852. <http://docsouth.unc.edu/southlit/simms/simms.html>

———. *The Wigwam and the Cabin. By the Author of "The Yemassee," "Guy Rivers," &c. First Series.* 1845. <http://docsouth.unc.edu/southlit/simmscabin1/simmscabin1.html>

Sinche, Bryan. "Godly Rebellion in *The Bondwoman's Narrative*." Gates and Robbins 175–91.

Smith, H. Shelton. *In His Image, But . . . . : Racism in Southern Religion, 1780–1910.* Durham, N.C.: Duke University Press, 1972.

Smith, Theophus. *Conjuring Culture: Biblical Formations of Black America.* New York: Oxford University Press, 1994.

Spencer, Anne. "Before the Feast of Shushan." *The Book of American Negro Poetry.* Ed. James Weldon Johnson. New York: Harcourt, Brace & Co., 1922. 213–15.

Staley, Susie C. *Holy Boldness: Women Preachers' Autobiographies and the Sanctified Self.* Knoxville: University of Tennessee Press, 2002.

Stanton, Elizabeth Cady. *The Woman's Bible: A Classic Feminist Perspective.* Mineola, N.Y.: Dover Publications, 2003.

Stauffer, John. "The Problem of Freedom in *The Bondwoman's Narrative*." Gates and Robbins 53–68.

Stave, Shirley A., ed. *Toni Morrison and the Bible: Contexted Intertextualities.* New York: Peter Lang Publishing, 2006.

Stein, Stephen J. "America's Bibles: Canon, Commentary, and Community." *Church History* 64.2 (June 1995): 169–84.

Stewart, Maria W. *Meditations.* Houchins, *Spiritual Narratives.*

———. *Productions of Mrs. Maria W. Stewart.* 1835. Houchins, *Spiritual Narratives.*

———. *Religion and the Pure Principles of Morality, The Sure Foundation on Which We Must Build*. Richardson 28–42.

Strange, Lisa S. "Pragmatism and Radicalism in Elizabeth Cady Stanton's Feminist Advocacy: A Rhetorical Biography." Diss. Indiana University, 1998.

Tanner, Benjamin Tucker. *An Apology for African Methodism*, 1867. <http://docsouth.unc.edu/church/tanner/tanner.html>

Tate, Claudia. *Domestic Allegories of Political Desire: The Black Heroine's Text at the Turn of the Century*. New York: Oxford University Press, 1996.

Taylor-Guthrie, Danielle. *Conversations with Toni Morrison*. Jackson: University Press of Mississippi, 1994.

Theological Dictionary of the New Testament. Ed. Gerhard Kittle and Gerhard Friedrich. Trans. Geoffrey W. Bromiley. Grand Rapids, Mich.: Eerdmans Academic Press, 1985.

Thiselton, Anthony C. "New Testament Historical Interpretation in Historical Perspective." *Hearing the New Testament: Strategies for Interpretation*. Ed. Joel B. Green. Grand Rapids, Mich.: Eerdmans Academic Press, 1995.

Towner, Lawrence. "The Sewall-Saffin Dialogue on Slavery." *William and Mary Quarterly* 21.1 (January 1964): 9–13.

Vanhoozer, Kevin J. *Is There a Meaning in This Text?* Grand Rapids, Mich.: Zondervan, 1998.

Walker, David. *Appeal in Four Articles, Together with a Preamble, to the Coloured Citizens of the World, But in Particular and Very Expressly to Those of the United States of America*. Boston: David Walker, 1830.

Walther, Malin LaVon. "Out of Sight: Toni Morrison's Revision of Beauty." *Black American Literature Forum* 24.4 (Women Writers Issue, Winter 1990): 775–89.

Washington, James Melvin, ed. *Conversations with God: Two Centuries of Prayers by African Americans*. New York: Amistad Press, 1995.

Weems, Renita. "Reading Her Way through the Struggle." Felder, *Stony the Road We Trod*, 57–80.

Wesley, Samuel. *The History of The Old And New Testament, Attempted in Verse*. Whitefish, Mont.: Kessinger Publishing, 2007.

Westerman, Claus. *Blessing in the Bible and the Life of the Church*. Trans. Keith Crim. Philadelphia: Fortress Press, 1968.

Wheatley, Phillis. "A Mother's Prayer for the Child in Her Womb." Washington 7.

Wiley, Calvin Henderson. *Alamance; Or, the Great and Final Experiment*. 1847. <http://docsouth.unc.edu/nc/wiley/wiley.html>

Williams, Adebayo. "Of Human Bondage and Literary Triumphs: Hannah Crafts and the Morphology of the Slave Narrative." *Research in African Literatures* 34:1 (Spring 2003): 137–50.

Williams, Delores. *Sisters in the Wilderness: The Challenge of Womanist God-Talk*. Maryknoll, N.Y.: Orbis, 2004.

Williams, Patricia J. *The Alchemy of Race and Rights: Diary of a Law Professor*. Cambridge, Mass.: Harvard University Press, 1991.

Williams, Peter, Jr. "A Prayer for Africa's Children." Washington 17.

Williams, Sherley Anne. *Dessa Rose*. New York: HarperCollins, 1999.
Willis, Deborah, ed. *Picturing Us: African American Identity in Photography*. New York: New Press, 1996.
Wilson, Adrian, and Joyce Lancaster Wilson. *A Medieval Mirror*. Berkeley: University of California Press, 1984.
Wilson, Harriet E. *Our Nig; or, Sketches from the Life of a Free Black*. Ed. Henry Louis Gates Jr. New York: Vintage Books, 1983.
Wimbush, Vincent L., ed. *African Americans and the Bible: Sacred Texts and Social Textures*. New York: Continuum, 2000.
———, ed. *Theorizing Scriptures: New Critical Orientations to a Cultural Phenomenon*. New Brunswick, N.J.: Rutgers University Press, 2008.
Wintersteen, Prescott B. *Christology in American Unitarianism*. Boston: Unitarian Universalist Christian Fellowship, 1977.
Wyatt, Jean. "Giving Body to the Word: The Maternal Symbolic in Toni Morrison's *Beloved*." *PMLA* 108.3 (May 1993): 474–88.
Yamauchi, Edwin M. *Africa and the Bible*. Grand Rapids, Mich.: Baker Academic Books, 2004.
Yellin, Jean Fagan. *Women and Sisters: The Antislavery Feminists in American Culture*. New Haven: Yale University Press, 1989.
Zizek, Slavoj. *Did Somebody Say Totalitarianism?* London: Verso, 2001.
Zonana, Joyce. "Feminist Providence: Esther, Vashti, and the Duty of Disobedience in Nineteenth-Century Hermeneutics." Hawley 228–49.

index of scriptural references

GENESIS
1:22 17
1:28 17
2:4–3:24 .... 62–63, 65, 108
3:1 34
3:16 .... 15, 95
3:17–19 15
3:19 123
4:1–16 14
9–10 86
9:22–25 33–34
12 65
15 65
16 17
21 17
32:24–28 113
37:1–36 79
37–41 81–83
40:5 85
40:8 84
40:14–15 83–84
40:23 85
49 18

EXODUS 119
7:13–14 .... 62, 108
8:15 .... 62, 108
8:19 .... 62, 108
8:32 .... 62, 108
9:7 .... 62, 108
9:12 .... 62, 108
9:34–35 .... 62, 108
12:12–13 76
12:29–30 119
14:8 .... 62, 108
23:16 .... 63, 110
26:33–34 .... 62, 109
29:36–37 .... 62, 109
30:10 .... 62, 109
31:8 .... 63, 65, 110
32:32 115
34:6–7 123
34:9 .... 63, 109
34:22 .... 63, 109
40:10 .... 62, 109

LEVITICUS
2:3 .... 62, 109
2:10 .... 62, 109
4:29–31 76
6:17 .... 62, 109
6:25 .... 62, 109
6:29 62
7:1 .... 62, 109
7:6 .... 62, 109
10:12 .... 62, 109
10:17 62
11:45 126
14:13 .... 62, 109
21:22 .... 62, 109

24:9	62, 109
24:29	109
27:28	62, 109

NUMBERS

6:24–26	63, 109
14:19	63, 109
22–24	3–4, 9
22:24–34	6
22:27–28	8
22:31	8–9
22:38	41
23:3	41
23:5	9
23:8	41
23:11	41
24:5	10
31:8	9

DEUTERONOMY

1:17	128
4:24	123
9:23	123
16:19	128
23:5	12
24:17	130
29:28–29	12
30:1–3	12

1 KINGS

1:2–4	74
8:27	57
8:57	130
19:1–13	73

2 KINGS

2:9	122

2 CHRONICLES

9:1–12	73
19:7	128

EZRA

42:13	109

ESTHER

1:16–19	72
2:10	72

JOB

9:12	115
14:1	124
15:15–16	123
19:25	56
29:14	127
37:22	123

PSALMS

5	56
8:3–4	123
14	62
19:9	112
22:1	76
25:11	63, 109
27:9	130
27:10	130
31:20	127
37:9	122, 129
39:7	114
50:1	121
51:9	116, 121
51:17	115
55:9	127
66:18	62, 109
67:1	63, 110
68	139n13
68:31	63, 111
73:18	118
75:6–7	128
78:36	127
79:5	118
80:3	63, 109
80:7	109
80:14	109
80:19	109
85:5	118
85:8	116
106:4	63, 110
110:1	113

113:3 121
119:37 118
119:135 ..... 63, 110
132:7 113
132:16 121
140:3 127

PROVERBS 111
21:1 118
24:23 128
26:22 74
26:25 74
28:21 128
31 69

SONG OF SONGS 19–22
1:5 ..... 19–20, 101
1:6 70
2:7 19
3:5 19
4:2–5 98
4:9–11 98
4:12–15 6
4:12–16 96
5:16 19
6:10–16 98
7:8 96
8:12 96

ISAIAH
6:2 112
6:2–3 60
6:9–10 ..... 62, 108, 119
9:1 ..... 139n13
29:13 ..... 62, 108
52:8 ..... 108, 114
52:58 62
55:8–9 130
58:6 121
59:1–2 116
61:10 127
62:6 108
66:1 ..... 113, 115

JEREMIAH
6:1 114
6:14 ..... 62, 108
6:17 108
8:12 ..... 62, 108
31:6 ..... 108, 114

EZEKIEL
20:13 62
20:16 62
20:21 62
20:24 62
37:1–14 ..... 63, 65, 110
42:13 62

DANIEL
4:35 115
9:17 ..... 63, 110

HOSEA
4:6 122

AMOS
4:11 ..... 117, 125
6:1 122

HABBAKUK
2:2–3 78
3:17 56

ZECHARIAH
3:2 ..... 117, 125
9:10 116

MALACHI
3:17 113–14

MATTHEW
3:9 ..... 63, 110
5:35 115
5:44 ..... 54, 127
6:9 115
6:9–10 108
8:2–3 121

9:12 121
9:20 45
9:20–21 75
10:42 126
11:28 65
13:13–17 .... 62, 108
13:13–27 119
15:8 .... 62, 109
15:14 .... 62, 108
15:21–28 .... 137n30
22:44 113
24:31 120
25:26 46

MARK
1:40–41 121
2:17 121
7:6 .... 62, 109
7:24–30 .... 137n30
7:25 46
7:27 46
9:41 126
12:36 113
15:25 46
28:19 35

LUKE
5:12–13 121
5:31 121
6:27 127
7:37–38 75
11:11 39
20:43 113
   43 116
   44 76

JOHN
6:68 113
13 75–76
15 75
15:5 .... 59, 118
15:13 76
20:27 124

ACTS
2:35 113
2:47 122
3:25–26 18
7:49 115
10:34 128
14:22 124
20:27 114

ROMANS
2:10 128
7:4 125
7:22 122
8:29 77
14:16 127

1 CORINTHIANS
3:6 118
3:16 59
9:24–25 61
9:25 .... 60, 128
13:13 92
13:22 6

2 CORINTHIANS
3:6 13
3:18 48
4:4 .... 62, 108, 119
4:16 122
5:1 .... 60–61, 128
8:9 119
12:2 57

GALATIANS
3:1 18
3:8-9 18
4:4 .... 139n13
5:22–23 126
6:16 129

EPHESIANS
1:3 18
1:7 117

2:7 117
3:16 122
3:20 114
4:13 56
6:9 128

PHILIPPIANS
4:13 59
4:19 124

COLOSSIANS
3:25 128

1 THESSALONIANS
4:16–17 120

1 TIMOTHY
1:17 .... 60, 112
2:4 .... 63, 111, 125
6:7–8 61
6:18 .... 60, 128

TITUS
2:10 126

HEBREWS
1:13 113
8:12 116
10:13 113
12:29 123
13:5 130

JAMES
2:1 128
2:5 .... 60, 128
2:9 128

1 PETER
1:3–4 61
1:4 .... 60, 128
1:15–16 126
1:17 128
1:18 126
2:12 126
3:1–2 126
3:4 126
5:5 .... 63, 111, 125

2 PETER
1:20–21 27
3:9 125

JUDE 9

REVELATION
1:8, 11 58
3:5 116
4:8 .... 60, 112
5:9 .... 63, 111, 119
7:1 120
7:9 .... 111, 119–20
7:9–12 .... 63, 111
7:13–14 76
8:3 63
8:3–4 .... 65–66, 110
8:4 63
14:6 .... 63, 111, 119
17:7 112
19:8 127
19:20 112
19:29 117
20:10 117
20:14–15 117
21:8 117
22:18–19 32

general index

Abraham cycle, blessing (*barak*) motif in, 17
Address to Miss Phillis Wheatley (Hammon), 55
African American Christians: as covenant people of Bible, 65; preliminary prayer practice of, 53–54; as unfree or underground, 35
African Americans and the Bible (Wimbush), 2
African American spirituals, 99–100
agency and desire, in *Dessa Rose*, 97
"Agency of the Letter in the Unconscious" (Lacan), 19–20, 22
Alchemy (Patricia Williams), 90–91
allegory, 19–22, 28–29, 32–33, 65, 89, 101–2, 105
Allen, Richard, "A Prayer for Hope," 56
Alter, Robert, 2, 9, 40–51, 93
AME (African Methodist Episcopal) church, 8, 10–11, 37, 56
American Bible, An (Gutjahr), 25–26
American Bible Society (ABS), 37–40
American Christians: and ascriptive Bible reading, 41; and church's dismissal of slaveholder, 44
American ideal of family, 87
American Missionary Association (AMA), 38
American Telescopes (Lawrence), 10

American Tract Society (ATS), 38
"America's Bibles" (Stein), 25–27
America's God (Noll), 2, 28–29, 31
Andrews, William, 11
anti-Semitism, and double-fall concept, 15, 134n12
antislavery poetry, 42–47
Apology for African Methodism (Tanner), 10
Appeal (David Walker), 4, 58, 64, 81
Autobiography of an Ex-Colored Man (James Weldon Johnson), 67, 70

"Balaam and His Master" (Harris), 10
Balaam trope, 6; and African American public hermeneutics, 40–42; black women's use of, 2, 10; context of, 9–10; linked to *Song of Songs*, 19–22; McMahon's derision of, 10; and Queen of Sheba, 74
barak. See blessing (*barak*)
beauty, and blackness, 19–20, 73, 102–4
"Before the Feast of Shushan" (Spencer), 72
Begrimed and Black (Hood), 14
Beloved (Morrison), 101–2, 105
Bibb, Henry, 3, 38–40
Bible: African American approach to, 12–13, 86–87; black/beautiful translations, 20, 103; and black cultural formation, 13–14; black "proof-texting,"

Bible (continued)
52; black women writers' use of, 2, 4, 7, 13–16, 93; canon of, 25–26, 133n1; criticism of, 26; dialectical approach to, 13; as Great Code of Western literature/culture, 13; liberationist themes in, 17, 36; and reading practices, 17, 20, 36, 41; as tool of social domination, 1, 7, 14; Wisdom tradition, and blessing, 18; *Woman's Bible* (Stanton), 26–27

Bible defense of slavery, 2, 28–34, 43–45, 48–49, 137nn28–29

Bibles for Slaves campaign, 37–40

biblical allusions, in Wilson's *Our Nig*, 87–91

biblical contradiction, 12–13

biblical interpretation, 41

biblical literacy, 35–37

biblical numerology, 11

biblical scholarship, 10, 52, 58, 68, 70

blackness: and beauty, 19–20, 73, 102–4; and Christology, 20; and enslavement, 91; and gender, race, class, 95; as metaphor, for America, 71; moral interpretation of, 14, 89–91; New Hamite theory of, 15; and race fallacy, 71; and racialized hermeneutic, 31–32; in Wilson's *Our Nig*, 86, 89–91

black women: double/triple fall of, 15, 90; power/agency of, in *Song of Songs*, 94; as prayer leaders, 54, 58; as prophets/seers, 11–12; public speaking of, 41–43, 45, 51–52, 58; sexual victimization of, 16, 81; social standing of, 20–21, 55; as "taking a text," 10, 58, 68, 70

Blanchard, Jonathan, 44, 137n29

blessing (*barak*): conceptualization of, 12–13, 16–18; language of (*shalom*), 18; as motif in Abraham cycle, 17; as redirecting curse (*qalal*), 17, 100; three biblical types of, 18

Bluest Eye, The (Morrison), 87, 101

Bondwoman's Narrative (Crafts), 67–69, 83

Boyd, Melba Joyce, 42, 137nn24–25

Brief and Candid Answer, A (Saffin), 31

Brighter Coming Day, A (Foster), 42

Bronte, Charlotte: *Jane Eyre*, 72; *Villette*, 72

Brown, William Wells, *Clotel*, 24

Buell, Lawrence, 68–69

Cain, as marked by blackness, 14–15

Callahan, Allen Dwight, *Talking Book*, 2, 12–13, 39, 79

Cartwright, Samuel A., 33–34

censorship, by U.S. mail authorities, 58

Cheng, Anne Anlin, "Wounded Beauty," 103

Christology: and blackness, 20; as central to biblical narrative, 41–43, 137n27; of Craft, 75–77; of Harper, 44–46; of Morrison, 100; and "passing" narrative, 76–77

Cima, Gay Gibson, 82

Clarke, Adam, 33

Clotel (Brown), 24

Coker, Daniel, 57–58

Conjuring Culture (Theophus Smith), 2, 13, 26

Connor, Kimberly Rae, 11

Conversations (Morrison), 93

Conversations with God (Washington), 54–55

Cornelius, Janet D., *When I Can Read My Title Clear*, 35–36

Crafts, Hannah: *Bondwoman's Narrative*, 67–69, 83; on story of Esther, 4; use of scripture, 2, 4, 67–69

cross-gender identification, 82–83

curse (*qalal*): and biblical interpretations, 14; Hebraic concept of, 17; redirected into blessing (*barak*), 17; sexuality/desire seen as, 70, 81, 99

curse of Ham: blackness and slavery as, 71, 97; and proslavery hermeneutics, 86; rabbinic and Christian commentary on, 14; and racial ideology, 14–16; and social domination, 14–15

160   GENERAL INDEX

cursing and blessing dialectic, 12–13, 19
Cushing, Eliza, 72

Degler, Rebecca, 104
Deism, 135n2, 136n7
desire: and agency, 97–100; and sexuality, 15–16, 19, 49, 70, 81, 86, 96
Dessa Rose (Williams), 97–100
dialectic, 12–13, 19
Did Somebody Say Totalitarianism? (Zizek), 92
discourses of power, 12–13
"Doers of the Word" (Peterson), 35, 51
Domestic Allegories of Political Desire (Tate), 89
Douglass, Frederick: on Bible defense of slavery, 3; on Bibles for Slaves campaign, 38–39; distinguishes Christianity from slave holding, 39; *Heroic Slave*, 21; *Life and Times*, 10, 36; *North Star*, 43; views of scriptures, 36
dreams, as literary trope, 82, 84–85
dry bones allegory, 65
DuBois, W. E. B., *Souls of Black Folk*, 11, 21, 70
DuCille, Ann, 94–95

Earl, Riggins J., 3
Elaw, Zilpha, *Memoirs of the Life*, 21–22, 70
emblems, and antislavery poetry, 46
Enlightenment, and biblical hermeneutics, 26–27, 30–32, 136n7
epistemology, of black feminists, 20–21
eroticism, in *Song of Songs*, 94–95
Esther metaphor, as "passing" narrative, 72–73
Europe, racial ideology construction in, 14–15
Evening Thought, An (Hammon), 55
"Everyone One's Own Interpreter?" (Marsden), 30
exegesis: fanciful, 33–34; in Harper's poetic canon, 44; and letter/spirit interpretation, 29; literalistic and proslavery, 28–29, 32–33; radicalized, 31–32, 35

family disintegration, in Wilson's *Our Nig*, 86–91
Fauset, Jessie, *Plum Bun*, 70
Felder, Cain Hope, *Troubling Biblical Waters*, 13–14, 74, 79
feminism: and Enlightenment rationalism, 27; hermeneutics of, 16–17, 72–73
Fiorenza, Elizabeth Schussler, *Searching the Scriptures*, 16
First African American Baptist Church (Boston), 52
Foster, Frances Smith, *A Brighter Coming Day*, 42
Frederick Douglass the Colored Orator (Holland), 10
freedom, and literacy, 35
Frei, Hans W., 41
Frelinghuysen, Theodore, 38
Frye, Northrop, 1, 33–34

Garnet, Henry Highland, 39
Garrison, William Lloyd, 29, 52
Gates, Henry Louis, Jr., 67
gender: and bodily substitution, 82; marginalized in Genesis 38, 81
Gifts of Power (Jackson), 39
God's Trombones (James Weldon Johnson), 53–54, 62, 65
Golden Rule, and antislavery, 44
Graham, Maryemma, 42
Grant, Jacqueline, *White Women's Christ, Black Women's Jesus*, 16
Grimke, Archibald H., *Right on the Scaffold*, 21
Gutjahr, Paul, *An American Bible*, 25–26

Hagar's Daughter (Hopkins), 16
Hagar trope, 16–17
Hammon, Jupiter: *Address to Miss Phillis Wheatley*, 55; *An Evening Thought*, 55
Hannah trope, 71
Harlem Renaissance, 72

Harper, Fenton, 43
Harper, Frances E. W.: antislavery poetry of, 2–3, 41–47; on Esther story, 72
Harper, Mary, 43
Harris, Joel Chandler, "Balaam and His Master," 10
Haynes, Lemuel, "A Prayer for a New Birth," 56
Haywood, Chanta M., "Prophesying Daughters," 12
hermeneutics: allegorical, in *Song of Songs*, 19–22; and Bible defense of slavery, 28–34, 43–45; of Crafts, 68–69; cultural, 13–14, 31, 47, 51; and Enlightenment rationalism, 26–27, 30–32, 136n7; feminist, 16–17, 72–73; letter/spirit, 13, 29–30; literalism and proslavery exegesis, 28–29; literary sampling, 51–53, 55, 57–66; manipulative, and slavery debate, 28–29; metaphorical, of Jesus, 46; and narrativity, 42; and nuptial metaphor, 94; "othered," 20; and private interpretation, 27–28, 41, 52; proslavery, and curse of Ham, 86; public, 41; racialized, 25–47, 73; and reduction theory, 81; scripture/nature, 30; transformative, 18, 94; and "unscripturing" of slave masters, 36–37
Heroic Slave (Douglass), 21
Hohnarth, Alaina, 140n8
Holland, Frederic May, *Frederick Douglass the Colored Orator*, 10
"Holy Madness, A" (Kristeva), 19, 96–97
Hood, Robert, *Begrimed and Black*, 14
Hopkins, Pauline, *Hagar's Daughter*, 16
Houchins, Susan, 51
Hoyt, Thomas, Jr., "Interpreting Biblical Scholarship," 52
Hurston, Zora Neale, *Their Eyes Were Watching God*, 2, 8

"Image of the United States" (Noll), 41–42
Incidents in the Life of a Slave Girl (Jacobs), 2, 82
In His Image (H. Shelton Smith), 33
"Interpreting Biblical Scholarship" (Hoyt), 52

Jackson, Rebecca Cox, *Gifts of Power*, 39
Jacobs, Harriet, *Incidents in the Life of a Slave Girl*, 2, 82
Jane Eyre (Bronte), 72
Jea, John, *Life, History and Unparalleled Suffering*, 21
Jefferson, Thomas: *Life and Morals of Jesus of Nazareth*, 26; *Philosophy of Jesus*, 26
Jeffrey, David Lyle, *People of the Book*, 11–12
Jenkins, William Sumner, 31, 33
Jobling, David, 81
Johnson, James Weldon: *Autobiography of an Ex-Colored Man*, 67, 70; *God's Trombones*, 53–54, 62, 65
Johnson, Thomas Lewis, *Twenty-eight Years a Slave*, 39
Jones, Absalom, "Thanksgiving Prayer," 56
Jordan, Winthrop D., *White Over Black*, 31
Joseph cycle, 79, 81–91
Judaism, on Ham/Canaan, 14–15

Kermode, Frank, 2, 9
Kern, Kathi, 27
Kort, Wesley A., *Take, Read*, 27, 30, 40
Kristeva, Julia, "A Holy Madness," 19, 96–97

Lacan, Jacques, "Agency of the Letter in the Unconscious," 19–20, 22
LaCocque, Andre, 20, 95–96
Landy, Francis, 98
language: of blessing, 18–19; political, 57–58, 62–64; from representation to embodiment, 93–94; in Shulamite trope, 19–22
Lawrence, Joshua, *American Telescopes*, 10

Lee, Jarena: and cross-gender identification, 82–83; licensed by AME Church, 8, 10–11; "Prayer for Sanctification," 57; *Religious Experience and Journal*, 3, 8, 10
Life and Morals of Jesus of Nazareth, The (Jefferson), 26
Life and Times (Douglass), 10, 36
Life, History and Unparalleled Suffering (Jea), 21
Life on the Old Plantation (Lowery), 9–10
literacy: abolitionist views of, 38; as linked to freedom and religion, 35–36; against proslavery hermeneutics, 39
literal/literalistic/allegorical interpretation, and proslavery exegesis, 28–29, 32–33
literary genres: essay, 53, 138n3; prayer, 53–58
literary sampling, and religious culture, 51–53, 55, 57–66
Lorde, Audre, 35
love: as antidote to death, 96; varieties of, 93–105
Lowery, Irving E., *Life on the Old Plantation*, 9–10
Luther, Martin, on Shulamite trope, 20

MacMahon, T. W., review of *Uncle Tom's Cabin*, 10
marriage: as denied to African Americans, 94–95; metaphors for, 95; and "passing," 72–73, 75–76
Marsden, George, "Everyone One's Own Interpreter?" 30
maternity: and *partus sequitur ventrem*, 16, 89, 101; in Wilson's *Our Nig*, 89–91
matriarchal/intergenerational trope, 18
Matter, E. Ann, *Voice of My Beloved*, 19
May, Cedric, 2, 51
McCaine, Alexander, *Slavery Defended from Scripture*, 33
méconnaissance, 76, 86, 103
Meditations (Stewart), 51–53

Memoirs of the Life (Elaw), 21–22, 70
Mercy, A (Morrison), 105
Moody, Joycelyn, *Sentimental Confessions*, 2, 11, 51, 54–55
Morrison, Toni, 35; allegory in *Beloved*, 101–2, 105; biblicism of, 2, 4, 93–94, 100; *The Bluest Eye*, 87, 101; *Conversations*, 93; "lethal maternity" theme of, 101; *A Mercy*, 105; *Playing in the Dark*, 78; *Song of Solomon*, 16, 100–105; *Tar Baby*, 101–3

narrative: and Christology, 41–43, 75–77, 137n27; Crafts's *Bondwoman*, 67–69, 83; of marriage and "passing," 72–73, 75–76; as transformative, 94
nature, as scripture, 31–32, 135–36n7
"New Testament Interpretation" (Thiselton), 28
Noll, Mark A.: *America's God*, 2, 28–29, 31; "Image of the United States," 41–42
North Star (Douglass), 43

orality, and literacy, 35
Origen, on Shulamite trope, 20
Our Nig (Wilson), 4, 81, 83, 85–86

partus sequitur ventrem law: and status of children, 3, 13, 16, 71; in Williams's *Dessa Rose*, 101; in Wilson's *Our Nig*, 83–84, 89–91
patriarchy, 18, 95
Patterson, Orlando, 16
Paul, R. Thomas, 52
Payne, Daniel Alexander, "Prayer for Dedication of a Church Edifice," 57
People of the Book (Jeffrey), 11–12
Peterson, Carla, 64; *"Doers of the Word,"* 35, 51; on Harper's poetry, 42
Philosophy of Jesus, The (Jefferson), 26
Pierce, Yolanda, 2
Plato, Ann, 138n3
Playing in the Dark (Morrison), 78
Plum Bun (Fauset), 70

Pocock, Judy, 101
poetry: biblical, in Stewart's prayers, 62, 110–18, 121–24, 127, 129–31; of Harper, 41–47, 49; metacritical, in *Song of Songs*, 19
political language, 57–58, 62–64
polygenesis, Jefferson's view of, 26
power: and agency, in *Song*, 94; and sight/insight, 11; of spoken word, 12
"Prayer for a New Birth, A" (Haynes), 56
"Prayer for Dedication of a Church Edifice" (Payne), 57
"Prayer for Hope, A" (Allen), 56
"Prayer for Sanctification" (Lee), 57
prayer genre: links sampling and biblical canon, 61–68; as literary/performative, 51–58, 61–66, 138–39n8; and political language, 57–58
prayer leaders, 54, 58
preaching: Lee, on women's right to, 10; prohibited for black women, 58, 68; as style of Crafts's work, 68
priestly/intercessory trope, 18
Productions (Stewart), 51, 53
prophecy, as gender-specific, 12
"Prophesying Daughters" (Haywood), 12
prophetic blessing, 18
prophetic discourse, 12–13
prophetic/interventional trope, 18
prophets/seers, 11–12

Queen of Sheba, and racial identity, 73–74

Race Music (Ramsey), 52
racism/racial ideology: and Bible defense of slavery, 28–45; and Crafts's identity and work, 67–68, 70–72; and cultural hermeneutics, 31; and curse of Ham, 14–16; and double-fall concept, 15, 134n9; and mark of Cain, 14–15; in Morrison's *Bluest Eye*, 102; northern, and de facto slavery, 81; polygenesis theory for, 26; Sewall-Saffin pamphlet debate on, 80; in Wilson's *Our Nig*, 86–91. See also *partus sequitur ventrem* law
Ramsey, Guthrie, *Race Music*, 52
rape, and *partus sequitur ventrem*, 16, 89–91
rationalism. *See* Enlightenment
"Reading *Her Way* Through the Struggle" (Weems), 17
reading practices, 17, 20, 36, 41
Reason, Charles L., 39
religion, and literacy, 2, 35–36
Religion and Pure Principals of Morality (Stewart), 52, 59, 61
Religious Experience and Journal (Lee), 3, 8, 10
Renaissance Bible (Shuger), 2
rhetoric, and literary sampling, 51–53, 55, 57–66
Rice, N. L., 44
Richards, Phillip, 79
Richardson, Marilyn, 51, 54–55, 58
Ricoeur, Paul, 2, 19–20, 41, 71, 94
Right on the Scaffold (Grimke), 21
Roach, Joseph, 82
Rohrbach, Augusta, 69

Saffin, John, *A Brief and Candid Answer*, 31
sampling. *See* literary sampling
Sancho, Ignatius, 10
scripture: definitions of, 27; postmodern view of, 30; in prayer-poems, 53–57; sampling of, by Stewart, 58–66; transforming of, 48–49. See also Bible
Searching the Scriptures (Fiorenza), 16
Selling of Joseph (Sewall), 79–80
Sentimental Confessions (Morrison), 2, 11, 51, 54–55
serpent, as black gardener, 34
Sewall, Samuel, *Selling of Joseph*, 79–80
sexuality and desire: as curse for black women, 70, 81, 86; and decriminalization of rape, 15–16; in *Dessa Rose*, 97–100; in Morrison's works, 104–5;

and Shulamite trope, 49, 97–100; and *Song of Songs*, 19, 94–96
shalom, as language of blessing, 18–19
Shuger, Debora, *Renaissance Bible*, 2
Shulamite trope, 3–4, 7, 19–22; in Crafts' work, 70–77; major themes of, 96; in Morrison's novels, 100–101; and Queen of Sheba, 74; sexuality/desire in, 49, 97–100; translations of black/beautiful, 20. See also *Song of Songs*
sight/insight, and analysis of power relations, 11
Simon of Cyrene trope, 42, 136n22
Sinche, Bryan, 68
Sisters in the Wilderness (Delores Williams), 17
slave missions movement, 34–35, 37
slavery, 16: and Balaam trope, 10; biblical defense of, in America, 7; Crafts's portrayal of, 67; as dehumanizing curse, 71, 97; historical sanction for, 31; and Joseph story, 79–80; northern indenture system, 83, 85; as oppression, 137n29; public debates about, 137nn24–25; Sewall's pamphlet against, 79–80; as socially constructed, 15–16. See also Bible defense of slavery; *partus sequitur ventrem* law
Slavery Defended from Scripture (McCaine), 33
Smith, H. Shelton, *In His Image*, 33
Smith, Theophus, *Conjuring Culture*, 2, 13, 26
Smyth, Thomas, on "double fall" of Ham's descendants, 15
social analysis, in Stewart's prayer genre, 64–65
social disenfranchisement, and alternative vision/insight, 11
social domination, and response to, 1, 7, 10–11, 13–16
social standing: of black women, 20–21, 55; and "curse of Ham," 14–15
Solomon, and Queen of Sheba, 74

Song of Solomon (Morrison), 16, 100–105
Song of Songs: allegorical signification of, 19–22; eroticism and blessing in, 94–95; major themes of, 96; and markers of blackness, 95; as metacritical genre, 19; as poem of desire/selfhood, 96; as prototype for *Dessa Rose*, 97–98; translation mutations of, 96. See also Shulamite trope
Souls of Black Folk (DuBois), 11, 21, 70
Spencer, Anne, "Before the Feast of Shushan," 72
spirituality: in black women's writings, 134n9; of Stewart, 51
spoken word, in religious history, 12, 35
Stanton, Elizabeth Cady, *Woman's Bible*, 26–27, 72
Stauffer, John, 67
Stave, Shirley A., 100
Stein, Stephen J., "America's Bibles," 25–27
Stewart, Maria W.: as America's first black woman political writer, 51; expressive mode of, and scripture, 2, 55–56, 107–31; law/grace problem and agency, 64; lectures mixed-gender audience, 52; *Meditations*, 51–53; political language of, 62–64; prayer-poems of, and scripture, 4, 51–58, 107–30; *Productions*, 51, 53; *Religion and Pure Principals of Morality*, 52, 59, 61
Stowe, Harriet Beecher, 10, 72
Syrophenecian Woman trope, 45–46

Take, Read (Kort), 27, 30, 40
Talking Book (Callahan), 2, 12–13, 39, 79
talking mule trope. *See* Balaam trope
Tanner, Benjamin, *Apology for African Methodism*, 10
Tar Baby (Morrison), 101–3
Tate, Claudia, *Domestic Allegories of Political Desire*, 89
"Thanksgiving Prayer" (Jones), 56
Their Eyes Were Watching God (Hurston), 2, 8

Theorizing Scriptures (Wimbush), 2, 25
Thiselton, Anthony E., "New Testament Interpretation," 28
Trappe (fictional slave catcher), 74
Troubling Biblical Waters (Felder), 13–14, 74, 79
Turner, Nat, 3, 35
Twenty-eight Years a Slave (Thomas Lewis Johnson), 39
Types of Man numerology, 11

Unitarianism, and Bible criticism, 26
United States, as "biblical nation," 41–42

VanHoozer, Kevin J., 32–33
Vesey, Denmark, 21, 35
Villette (Bronte), 72
vision/supernatural sight, 11
Voice of My Beloved (Matter), 19

Walker, David, 3, 35, 52; *Appeal*, 4, 58, 64, 81
Walker, Madame C. J., 103
Walther, Malin LaVon, 103
Ward, Samuel Ringhold, 39
Washington, James Melvin, *Conversations with God*, 54–55
Washington, Madison, 21
Watkins, William, 43
Watkins, William J., 43
Weems, Renita, "Reading *Her Way* Through the Struggle," 17

Weld, Theodore, 33
Westerman, Claus, 12, 17–19
Wheatley, Phillis, 55–56
When I Can Read My Title Clear (Cornelius), 35–36
White Over Black (Jordon), 31
White Women's Christ, Black Women's Jesus (Grant), 16
Williams, Adebayo, 67
Williams, Delores, *Sisters in the Wilderness*, 17
Williams, Patricia, *Alchemy*, 90–91
Williams, Peter, Jr., 57
Williams, Sherley Ann: biblicism of, 2, 4, 94; *Dessa Rose*, 97–100
Wilson, Harriet W., 4; approach of, to scripture, 2; *Our Nig*, 4, 81, 83, 85–86
Wimbush, Vincent L.: *African Americans and the Bible*, 2; *Theorizing Scriptures*, 2, 25
Woman's Bible (Stanton), 26–27, 72
Woman with Alabaster Box, 75
Woman with Issue of Blood trope, 45, 75
"Wounded Beauty" (Cheng), 103
Wyatt, Jean, 102

Yamauchi, Edwin, 74
Yellin, Jean Fagan, 46

Zizek, Slavoj, *Did Somebody Say Totalitarianism?* 92
Zonna, Joyce, 72

www.ingramcontent.com/pod-product-compliance
Lightning Source LLC
Chambersburg PA
CBHW011753220426
43672CB00017B/2948